THE
KEEN FOXHUNTER'S
MISCELLANY

THE
KEEN FOXHUNTER'S
MISCELLANY

by

PETER HOLT

Quiller

Copyright © 2010 Peter Holt

First published in the UK in 2010
by Quiller, an imprint of Quiller Publishing Ltd

British Library Cataloguing-in-Publication Data
A catalogue record for this book
is available from the British Library

ISBN 978 1 84689 065 9

Printed in Malta by Gutenberg Press Ltd.
Book and jacket design by Sharyn Troughton.

Quiller
An imprint of Quiller Publishing Ltd
Wykey House, Wykey, Shrewsbury, SY4 1JA
Tel: 01939 261616 Fax: 01939 261606
E-mail: info@quillerbooks.com
Website: www.countrybooksdirect.com

DEDICATION

For my dear lady wife whose name escapes me...

ACKNOWLEDGEMENTS

MY PARTICULAR THANKS go to Martin Scott, former Master and huntsman of the Tiverton and the VWH, and England's greatest hound expert, for his invaluable assistance in sub-editing this book. I am also grateful to my old friend Edward Foster, former Master of the Trinity Foot Beagles, the Wheatland and the South Shropshire, who gave me many helpful insights into the intricate business of hunting. Also, thanks to other hunting friends and acquaintances who have helped me, not least on the vexed topic of the colour of hunt livery, a subject that seems to cause alarmingly high blood pressure in hunting circles. I have discovered that to get the colour of the Heythrop huntsman's jacket wrong is regarded as simply heinous. It is green, not red. A truly terrifying mistake. I swear I will never do it again. So thank you to the various foxhunters who corrected the manuscript for errors and deleted some of the more dubious stories. Having experienced what can only be described as a Lord Haw-Haw moment with my first draft, I pray that the end result is reasonably palatable to all.

The Author and the Publishers are grateful to the following for permission to reproduce copyright material:

The Master of Foxhounds Association for permission to use various nuggets of advice including extracts from their booklet *Competencies Required Within A Mastership*; Alan Monckton for permission to reproduce the poem *The New Hunter*, by Francis Monckton; Roger Waters for permission to reprint the lyrics to the Pink Floyd song *Free Four*; Quiller Publishing for an exerpt from *A Manual of Foxhunting*, by Ronnie Wallace, (Swan Hill Press) 2003; *Country Life* for excerpts from *Crascredo* and *The Wag*, 1928, and the *Foxhunting Companion*, 1978; The Random House GroupLtd for an excerpt from *On Hunting* by Roger Scruton published by Yellow Jersey Press; the estate of the late Dick Francis for some of his splendid hunting reminiscences; David and Charles for permission to use exerpts from *Foxhunting*, by the Duke of Beaufort, 1988; Charles Moore for permission to use an extract from an article in *The Spectator*.

Every effort has been made to obtain permission to reproduce extracts but in some cases this has not been possible.

INTRODUCTION

'If any man could be justified in swearing,
it would be a Master of hounds'.

Anthony Trollope

WHEN MY PUBLISHER ANDREW JOHNSTON suggested I follow up my shooting book *The Keen Shot's Miscellany* with a similar treatise on hunting, I approached the project with extreme caution. Was I setting myself up for a modern day Bateman cartoon? The Shooting Man Who Dared To Write A Book About Hunting. One could imagine the furious, florid faces of the foxhunters; the mocking howl of the hounds; the fox's sneer.

But I did some research on hunting, talked it through with hunting friends, including my wife (an MFH, no less), and at the risk of feeling like an RAF Squadron Leader (engineering branch) going to dine with the officers of the Queen's Guard at St James's Palace, I decided that this could be fun. There were so many wonderful characters in hunting, so many good stories to be told. I reasoned that as an outsider I might find it easier to see the funny, sometimes ludicrous side to a great sport that has spent recent years tragically emasculated by a bad law.

I admit that I have never hunted. The closest I have got to hunting (apart from my wife) is to be a member of a gloriously anachronistic institution called The Shrewsbury Hunt Club. Founded in 1769 the Shrewsbury is England's second oldest surviving hunt club after the Tarporley in Cheshire. It is also England's least horsey hunt. The Shrewsbury has never owned its own pack nor even organised its own hunting. It once had an aim to promote foxhunting in Shropshire but a surfeit of good champagne caused that to be forgotten long ago.

These days the club is strictly social. Like myself, most of the 100 members do not hunt and many have barely met a horse. We meet only for a ball when we wear our uniform of blue coat with scarlet velvet collar, buff waistcoat, black silk breeches, black stockings and court shoes. Some might say it's pointless, but hell, you've got to try to enjoy yourself these days, haven't you?

A friend of mine, a senior member, recalls wearing the Shrewsbury uniform to a Hambledon Hunt ball. He ended up on the dance floor with one of the Hambledon's grand dames, a powerful Pony Club lady.

'And what is that uniform you are wearing?' she enquired over the pince nez, peering at his blue coat. 'Is it the Beaufort?'

'Aha, no, this is the Shrewsbury Hunt Club,' my friend replied brightly. 'We meet once a year for a dance. It's a bit of a joke really because we don't actually hunt'.

'Dance? Joke?' growled the grand lady. 'I find nothing in the slightest bit amusing about that'. And she swept off the floor in disgust.

Before I finish, and before the fluffies get in a lather, can I point out that some of the hunting practices mentioned in this book were done away with years ago. The Master of Foxhounds Association quite rightly outlawed bagged foxes shortly after its founding in 1881. Likewise, if you decide to follow the example of the eighteenth century foxhunting brandy merchant Thomas Philips, who requested in his will that he be placed in his coffin with a fox pad in each hand, your vicar is likely to have an apoplexy. Not to mention your friends, who would consider you exceedingly odd. And the extraordinary nineteenth century American practice of immersing a fox's foot in a glass of port in order to improve the taste cannot be condoned on any grounds, not least health and safety. Nor does it say much for the quality of your port.

IN THE BEGINNING...

THE BIBLE does not consider it wrong to hunt animals that attack man's domesticated animals. In the Old Testament (1 Samuel 17: 34-35) David, in his role as shepherd, had to kill a lion and a bear in order to protect his sheep. Nowhere in the Bible does it indicate that it is okay or not okay to hunt animals for sport, although Genesis states that animals were created for the benefit of man.

The most significant mention of foxes in the Bible appears in Judges 15: 4-5 when Samson lost his temper after learning that his wife had been given in marriage to his best man. In revenge he caught 'three hundred foxes; and he took torches, turned the foxes tail to tail, and put a torch between each pair of tails. When he had set the torches on fire, he let the foxes go into the standing grain of the Philistines, and burned up both the shocks and the standing grain, as well as the vineyards and olive groves.' The Philistines retaliated by burning Samson's wife and father-in-law. Samson then set about killing more Philistines and so it went on. The fuss over the hunting ban seems tame by comparison.

THE FIRST TALLY-HO

The first people to go hunting were the ancient Egyptians. Before 1500 BC they hunted on foot but then the horse arrived and everything changed. The horses of the Pharaohs were too small for long distance riding so Egyptian noblemen attached their steeds to lightweight chariots. Armed with javelins they would pursue lion, bull, stag, gazelle, wild sheep and hare. To start with, hunting was done in the desert but Egyptian huntsmen realised it was more fun to net their quarry and bring it back alive to gameparks where it could be hunted with hounds. Dogs, similar to today's greyhounds, were bred to follow scent. Mastiffs were turned on bigger quarry such as lions. Small terrier-like dogs were used for coursing hares. More adventurous nobles coursed with trained cheetahs. The Egyptians realised that they needed the kit as well. They designed hunting clothes. Mid-thigh tunics were replaced with knee-length costumes.

By the ninth century BC the Assyrians of Mesopotamia had inherited the Egyptians' obsession for hunting. Before a hunt prayers were said to King Nimrod – first Assyrian king after Noah's flood – who was worshipped by his followers as a 'mighty hunter before the Lord'. The Assyrians treated hunting as a military operation, a kind of conquest of animals.

Two centuries later King Assurbanipal of Assyria was hunting wild donkeys on horseback, a sport that became fairly dull as the horse developed and became quicker. The donkeys didn't stand a chance. The Persians copied the idea of gameparks from the Egyptians and Assyrians and their seventh century king Cyrus the Great introduced stag hunting and pig sticking. Cyrus spent his time hunting all over his kingdom, thus enabling him to keep an eye on his estates, a habit that was to become the basis of European hunting fifteen centuries later.

NOTHING MORE ENVIABLE

'There is no position in life more enviable or more enjoyable than that of a Master of Hounds in a good country; we may add, in almost any country. He is more independent than Her Majesty's Prime Minister of State and more regarded as a keeper of fox hounds than the Keeper of the Privy Seal'.

From Baily's Sporting Magazine, *1868*

THE JOYS OF DOUBLE NEGATIVES

'No one who has not conducted a pack of foxhounds on early morning exercise has tasted the joys of life to the full; no one who has not accompanied them has lived at all'.

David Brock, MFH, 1930.

PANIC

THERE WAS PANIC AMONGST THE FOXHUNTING COMMUNITY in 1969 with the news that a dog had been found with rabies in Camberley, Surrey. A rabies epidemic would have presented a grave danger to hunting since all movement of hounds would have been immediately banned. Government vets swarmed through the countryside around Camberley where they trapped and tested a large amount of wildlife. A number of urban foxes were shot. No more cases of the disease were found. It transpired that an Army officer had brought the dog into England from Germany. Despite the dog completing quarantine requirements, by a freak chance the disease had developed months later.

Rabies is transmitted to humans by bites or scratches from rabid foxes, bats, rats and domestic dogs and cats. The disease attacks the central nervous system leading to seizures. Once clinical signs such as frothing at the mouth occur there is no known cure and death is certain.

ESSENTIAL INFO FOR HOSTESSES

County personages were listed in order of rank by the legendary late nineteenth century MFH Lord Willoughby de Broke. This list tells the hostess who she should put on her right at a dinner party (in the absence of Royalty or aristocracy, of course). Please note that a Master of Fox Hounds is far more important than an MP. Takes little to work that one out!

> The Lord Lieutenant
> The Master of Foxhounds
> The Agricultural Landlords
> The Bishop
> The Chairman of the Quarter Sessions (the judge)
> The Colonel of the Yeomanry
> The Member of Parliament
> The Dean
> The Archdeacons
> The Justices of the Peace
> The lesser clergy
> The larger farmers

Note: It was a matter of debate as to whether the Lord Lieutenant should come at the top of this list. In some southern counties the MFH was considered far more important, and often more interesting.

• Richard Greville Verney, 19th Baron Willoughby de Broke was described by an acquaintance as 'a genial and sporting young peer, whose face bore a pleasing resemblance to the horse...he had quite a gift for writing, thought clearly, and was not more than two hundred years behind his time'. Young Richard decided early on that hunting would be the most important thing in his life. At Oxford in the 1890s de Broke was advised that he was capable of getting a first class degree if he was prepared to read seven hours a day. 'But how was I to hunt if I were to read seven hours a day?' he recalled. 'I could hunt once a week perhaps, in the afternoons.' This was out of the question. In the end he got a third.

• Lord Willoughby de Broke produced several books on hunting, the most notable being the *Hunting The Fox*, written in 1920 following the deprivations of the war years. De Broke complained, 'To ride a horse half-fit and to ride that horse all day; to hunt hounds that are poorly fed; to know that even if they were in good enough condition to tire their fox he would amost surely find an open earth; to be short-handed both in the hunting field and in the kennel; to have a diminishing number of walks for puppies – all these things have not made the management of hunting during the War a very pleasing occupation.'

WRONG WAY ROUND

HAVING PURCHASED AN ESTATE in Pytchley country, the new owner, some non-hunting industrialist or other, thought it was only polite to write to the Hunt to tell them his shooting dates for the next season. It was the 1950s and the pack was being led by a formidable lady MFH called Griselda Grant-Lawson. She returned the letter with a terse note scribbled on it: 'In the Pytchley, we send you our hunting dates…'

• 'Grizzy' Grant-Lawson is not the only MFH to have scrawled such a note. In some countries hunting took automatic precedence over shooting. While Ronnie Wallace was Master of the Heythrop, shoot owners were so terrified he would have them ostracised from Gloucestershire society that they would wait patiently for the Heythrop's meet list before setting their dates.

POOR CHARLES

CHARLES LENNOX, 4th Duke of Richmond, was a great sportsman who ended up as Governor General of Canada in 1818. Unfortunately Charlie got his own back on poor Charles. After only a year in office, the Duke died of rabies having been bitten by a pet fox belonging to one of his soldiers. He died in agony. A contemporary described how over four days Richmond 'developed pain in his throat, would not wash or shave, could only swallow with the greatest of difficulty, developed visible spasms in his throat and became increasingly agitated at the sight or even smell of water (hydrophobia).' The Duke's deathbed request was that his spaniel Blucher be given to his wife Mary. He added the sad warning, 'It will make her cry at first, but turn him in when she is alone and shut the door'.

• Colonel Charles Lennox was a bon vivant known for his drinking games. While hunting in Ireland towards the end of the eighteenth century he issued a challenge to the members of Benson's Club, made up of members from the Kildare Hunt Club. Lennox wagered that the Benson boys could not each drink two bottles of brandy, smoke an ounce of tobacco, dine on devilled kidneys, stay up all night and then spend the following day hunting. They managed to stay up all night getting plastered, but next day most of them had either pulled up or fallen off their mounts by noon. Only one, a Mr O'Reilly, managed to keep going with the colonel. The tiebreaker involved consuming the same quanties of brandy, tobacoo and kidneys but this time the contenders had to keep it up all week, drinking, smoking and hunting, from Monday through to Sunday. On Sunday morning, the colonel emerged on his knees from the hotel smoking room. He asked a skivvy where Mr O'Reilly was. He was pointed towards the hotel kitchen. There he was amazed to see his opponent dancing with a chambermaid. Lennox surrendered. He exclaimed, 'I never met a man before, who could drink six nights, hunt six days, and then enjoy an Irish jig with Betty'.

ROCKET FUEL

In the middle ages the traditional herbs for mixing with wine to make a stirrup cup – a brew that was drunk while astride your horse before saying farewell – were hyssop, rue and burnet.

The modern recipe for stirrup cup is sugar, lemon juice and equal measures of cognac and cherry brandy, mixed to individual taste and poured into your hip flask.

If you yearn for something stronger, try this ripsnorter of a sherbert that appears in a nineteenth century colonial manual called *Hints To Hunters, Sportsmen and Travellers* by H. A. Levenson, aka The Old Shekarry. Be warned that this hideous mixture is likely to make you behave so badly that the Master will send you home. Or you will feel so sick that you will want to go home:

Beat up the yokes of six eggs with half a pint of rum or brandy, three lumps of sugar, lemon peel cut thin, cloves and cardamon. Add a quart of milk, mix well and grate in nutmeg. Serves three. Have plenty of Alka Seltzer on standby.

• The Percy in Northumberland have their own stirrup cup known as a Percy Special which is designed to 'make fences look smaller'. It is concocted of abundant, equal measures of whisky and cherry brandy and nothing else. A visitor to the Percy commented, 'In the city, this would be called an alcohol problem; in the country, it is a tipple. I could not decide whether it made it more or less likely that the riders would fall off. It would certainly make it less likely they would notice if they did'.

• The Percy's neighbours, The West Percy, offer a derivative of the Percy Special known as the Hedgeley Special, named after the seat of the Carr-Ellison family, who have produced a long line of West Percy MFHs. This noxious fluid consists of two thirds Alnwick Rum and a third cherry brandy. In the words of one subscriber it is 'shamefully disgusting'. It will come as no surprise to foxhunters that this drink was invented by the one Carr-Ellison who preferred shooting to hunting. Alnwick Rum, a gut-thumping blend of rum from Jamaica and Guyana, was first produced in Northumberland during the First World War. It is ideally best drunk on a park bench.

TOM FIRR...

ONE OF THE GREATEST HUNTSMEN OF THEM ALL was Tom Firr of the Quorn (1872–97).

The son of an Essex Hunt kennelman, Firr cut his teeth as whipper-in with various packs including the Craven, the Tedworth and the Pytchley (where he achieved minor celebrity for taking part in the famous Waterloo Run of 1866.) Firr arrived at the Quorn aged forty-one under the Mastership of ship owner John Coupland, who as a young man in India had kept pack of hounds for hunting jackal on the outskirts of Bombay. Coupland's advantage was that he was extremely rich – he kept no less than twenty-five hunters in Quorn country.

During his twenty-five years at the Quorn, Firr transformed the hunt into England's greatest. Coupland's money ran out and the Quorn Mastership was eventually taken over by the 'Yellow Earl' Lord Lonsdale, who proceeded to lavish his iron-ore fortune on the hunt. Lonsdale saw to it that Firr and the hunt servants were the best turned out in England in their white leather breeches and dark red coats on chestnut thoroughbreds.

Despite the changes in Mastership, Firr remained a constant in the Quorn. Viscount Chaplin, Master of the Burton, said of Firr, 'No one could handle a big field better than he could, that I've ever seen; and the way in which he controlled a field of possibly five or six hundred horsemen on a Quorn Friday was a triumph of organisation I have never seen surpassed. For instance, when drawing one of their crack coverts in that country, the field was kept away some distance from it, often nearly a whole field, until the fox had gone away, and the huntsman had got hold of his hounds sufficiently to get a start of him; and then, when the field got the order to go, my word! There was a charge of cavalry with a vengeance to get up on them.'

The Field's hunting correspondent Brooksby couldn't wait to hunt with Firr. 'As Tom Firr's horn and scream brought hounds bounding out of covert a thrill would ram up one's very backbone. As he jammed the horn home – and invariably peeped at his watch – one knew that a gallop had begun and that joy was before us. While hunting a fox he seldom cared to have a whipper-in in attendance; his quiet "yo-oi" was enough to swing hounds to their cast and to stay the most fervent galloper. As the pack went forward anew, so did Firr with a heart-stirring cheer of endorsement, and apparently with the easiest piece in the fence exactly opposite him. Other great huntsmen there have been, but only one Tom Firr...'

Firr's hard riding got the better of him in the end. In 1897 a bad fall forced him to retire. He died of throat cancer in 1902 aged sixty-one.

Despite his working class background, Firr managed to complete nine years of school. His education allowed him to become an accomplished song writer and no hunt supper was complete without a few verses from the Quorn huntsman. His compositions were based on incidents he had seen while hunting. He also used verse to remind himself of hunting technique:

When approaching an obstacle, narrow or wide,
No matter how much you may be 'on the ride,'
Take a pull at your bridle, and shorten your stride,
Till the pack settle down to the scent t'other side.

OR FRANK FREEMAN...

There is much debate in the hunting world as to who was the better huntsman: Tom Firr of The Quorn or Frank Freman of the Pytchley (1906-1931.)

Unlike the outgoing Firr, Freeman was a dour, silent man known for his slow, rather sad smile. But while Firr may have won on personality and was the better horseman, many say that Freeman was a far superior huntsman. Indeed, the combination of Freeman under the Mastership of Lord Annaly at the Pytchley is said to have been about as good as you will get.

Freeman is often referred to as a genius. Of all his pack he was said to prefer small, active bitches and once remarked that he never knew of a hound breaking its leg due to it being light of bone. Those who hunted with him at the Pytchley could seldom recall a bad day and even on bad scenting days Freeman, known for his unusual cheering sounds and his low whistle when hunting hounds, would always get his fox even if he literally walked it to death. 'His hounds would always be hunting a fox and never Freeman,' reported a member of the Pytchley field. 'And the same cannot be said of every huntsman.'

Like Tom Firr before him, Freeman had hunting in his blood. He was born in 1876 at the Kildare Hunt kennels at Jigginstown, Ireland. His father was the English huntsman to Major Edmond Mansfield, Master of the Kildare. When Frank was one the family moved back to England. Freeman senior went to the North Hereford before moving on to the South and West Wilts and by the age of twelve Frank was riding second horse to his father. Aged eighteen, after a lacklustre career at Warminster Grammar School where he never let studying interfere with hunting, Frank got his first job, as whipper-in with the Tickham in Kent. After stints with the Brocklesby, the Kildare (where, he is said to have learned to gallop and to protect hounds from an ignorant, hard-riding field) the Belvoir, the North Cheshire, and the Bedale, he ended up at the Pytchley in 1906 at the age of thirty.

Freeman's biographer Guy Paget described the secrets of Frank's successs: 'He was bred and born to the game. He had fifteen years whole time professional experience before he became a huntsman. He weighed under ten stone. He was well built for a saddle; he had a good voice; he could wind a horn with any man. He was endowed with an iron nerve and a good courage – two very different things: nerve is the feeling you'll never fall, and courage the feeling that does not stop you when you know you will.'

Paget added, 'Where Freeman's genius was born or made no one can lay down… I would put Freeman's success down to his one-track mind, and the undoubted personal magnetism he had for his hounds. The joy of hunting with Freeman was not that the Pytchley had longer points or more great hunts than other packs, but that they had so astoundingly few bad days... Any huntsman can show good sport with a good fox on a good scent; genius comes in when a huntsman contrives, by fair means, an enjoyable day with all these requisites against him.'

Freeman retired in 1931. His final hunt, on 4 April at Harleston Heath, featured a special guest in the form of the four-year-old Princess Elizabeth, our future Queen, on her pony led by her mother.

Guy Paget was a member of the field that day. 'Soon a hound spoke, then another,' he wrote. 'In a minute a glorious dog fox jumped up on the stone wall bounding the covert. From there he took a look round, and seemed to bow to Their Royal Highnesses. I was afraid that we had headed him; but no, he jumped off, ran diagonally across our front not a hundred yards off, and the future Queen of England halloaed him away. With a crash of music, Freeman cantered over the wall with his pack, and away we went...'

Freeman died in 1947 aged 71.

FRENZY

'The magic for us is sometimes to be found in the sheer overpowering beauty of a single image: dappled sunlight on dappled hounds racing through woodland, or when standing on a hill at first light and hearing the cautious note of a single hound in the mist joined by more and more until the whole valley explodes in a frenzy of music.'

Baroness Mallalieu, Labour politician and hunt supporter

THE FIRST BEAGLER

Beagling began in fifth century BC Greece after farmers got fed up with horses trampling their crops. (Where have we heard that story before?)

The first beagler was the Athenian writer and soldier Xenophon. Intensive agriculture had forced the big game into the mountains. All that remained on the farmland were hares. So Xenophon took to his feet.

Xenophon developed a hound called the Castorian which was said to be a cross between a dog and a fox. His pack would hunt together, nose to the ground. Xenophon held strong views on breeding and training. He believed that the perfect hound should possess four important attributes: 'courage, sound feet, a keen nose, and a sleek coat'.

He wrote: 'The hound should be of large build...with a light small head, broad and flat in the snout, well knit and sinewy, the lower part of the forehead puckered into strong wrinkles; eyes set well up in the head, black and bright; forehead large and broad; the depression between the eyes pronounced; ears long and thin, without hair on the under side; neck long and flexible, freely moving on its pivot; chest broad and fairly fleshy...he will be strong in build, and at the same time light and active; they will have symmetry at once and pace; a bright, beaming expression; and good mouths'.

If the huntsman could produce a dog like this, then his hounds would 'show their mettle by rapidly quitting beaten paths, keeping their heads sloping to the ground, smiling, as it were to greet the trail. When they are close to the hare itself, they will make the fact plain to the huntsman by the quickened pace at which they run, as if they would let him know by their fury, by the motion of head and eyes, by rapid changes of gait and gesture, now casting a glance back and now fixing their gaze steadily forward to the creature's hiding-place, by twistings and turnings of the body, flinging themselves backwards, forwards, and sideways, and lastly, by the genuine exaltation of spirits, visible enough now, and the ecstasy of their pleasure, that they are close upon the quarry'. But most importantly, the hound should never be allowed to leave the scent 'and return crestfallen to the huntsman'.

REAR END

A stag has a 'tail', a buck has a 'single', a fox has a 'brush', a hound has a 'stern', a hare has a 'scut'.

In the middle ages a fox was sometimes described as having a 'bush'. In France the brush was used in church to sprinkle holy water so the old French for fox was goupil, hence the word goupillon for holy water sprinkler.

PRANK

THE FIRST ENGLISH-STYLE FOX HUNT in Ireland was the Kilkenny Hunt Club, founded in 1797 by a Tipperary man called John Power. The Kilkenny met in November and February and by the late 1820s the town of Kilkenny had become Ireland's answer to Melton Mowbray, though considerably rowdier. Vast quantities of booze were drunk in Rice's Hotel by squires, who competed with practical jokes. Most memorable prank concerned the Marquis of Waterford, who rode his horse up the brass-bound staircase into the Club Room (now part of the Club House Hotel), jumped the dining table, and returned the way he came.

The Kilkenny spawned other hunt clubs throughout Ireland of which the most famous was Robert Parsons Persse's pack in Galway known as the Blazers. Theories abound as to the origin of the name. One story relates that the pack were named after the red hair of two of its members; another has it that after a joint meet with the rival Ormond Hunt, Persse's followers set fire to the Master of the Ormond's house, hence the 'Blazers' tag.

ROMAN DAYS

The first mention of hounds 'speaking' is by the Roman poet Ovid. He refers to hounds that 'sniff the wind with raised heads, then lower their noses to the ground and speak to the line'.

The Romans were the first to blow hunting horns. By AD 180 they were using four foot metal trumpets to drive animals from coverts.

The first British hound was the Agassaean, a small, shaggy, barrel-bodied brute known for its good nose. The Romans discovered the dog when they arrived in Britain in AD 72.

NETTED

THE WORLD'S FIRST ORGANISED FOX HUNTS took place in Italy towards the end of the first century. At first the fox was netted at the end of the chase in order to protect the pelt. But critics saw that this was unfair on hounds. It didn't take long for the Italians to realise that foxhunting with a large pack of hounds with the fox dying at the end of the chase was the only way forward.

FLEETING AND TRANSIENT

'Though other nations boast keen sportsmen, and first-rate horsemen and shots amongst them, in England alone does the innate love of the chase appear to pervade the whole community. Let a fox be viewed, or the sound of the horn heard in the neighbourhood of any village, and straightway every man, woman, and child will turn out to see all they can, though experience must have taught the greater portion of them that their view of the spectacle will at most be but a fleeting and transient one.'

By J. Nevill Fitt, from Covert-Side Sketches, *1879*

HUNTING MAD

DR BENJAMIN RUSH (1745-1813) was one of America's Founding Fathers. He also had a good sense of humour well illustrated by a short piece he wrote about hunting.

Titled *The Hunting Mania*, it told the story of a mad man in England whose doctor had prescribed cold baths in order to cure his lunacy. One day, the mad man was taking a walk when he met the servant of the local hunting squire.

The mad man asked the servant how much it cost his master to maintain his horses and hounds.

'£500 a year,' the servant said.

'And how much does he sell his foxes for after he catches them?' asked the loony.

'For nothing at all,' the servant replied.

'For nothing!' the mad man said with astonishment. 'I wish my physician could see him – he would soon order him to use the cold bath…'

ONE AT A TIME

'We must not write of hunting in Ireland without any mention of the culminating rite that brings all fox-hunters together, which is the Hunt Ball. There you will see every member of the Hunt; and not to be present then, if you belong to the Hunt, is to be thought dead. On such occasions the light-blue facings of the Meath may be seen varied by the white facings of their neighbours the Kildare, the French-grey facings of their northern neighbours the Louth, and the black collar and white facings of the Westmeath, with the single fox on the left lapel; all these facings, of course, on red coats. And if anyone ask a member of the Westmeath why his lapels do not match, or whether he has lost a badge, he or she will find the answer lurking, all ready to leap out, that the Westmeath only hunt one fox at a time…'

From My Ireland, by *Lord Dunsany, Funk & Wagnalls, 1937*
(Dunsany, was an Irish peer and writer famous for his fantasy short stories)

POLITICAL POLICE

Foxhunters were angry in 2009 when they heard that an animal rights group was secretly training Cumbria police officers to help them enforce the hunting ban. This explained why the Blencathra, one of Britain's oldest hunts, was being regularly followed by dozens of police who might have been better employed catching burglars in Barrow-in-Furness. Cumbria Chief Constable Craig Mackey asked the International Fund for Animal Welfare to teach his officers how to spot illegal hunting. IFAW jumped at the chance.

• Thames Valley Police underwent similar anti hunting 'training' with the League Against Cruel Sports.

• Much to the relief of foxhunters and coppers, the police announced in May 2009 that they would stop monitoring hunts who might be breaking the law. New guidance from the Association of Chief Police Officers stated that gathering evidence of illegal hunting was difficult and that the ban was hard to enforce. Chief Constables had more pressing priorities. ACPO added that in future forces should rely on anti-hunt activists to produce information, but they should be 'very cautious' of such groups who were likely to be infiltrated by ' militants' – i.e. headbangers accustomed to telling outrageous porkies. In a historic moment of police enlightenment, Richard Brunstrom, Chief Constable of North Wales and ACPO spokesman on rural affairs, said: 'Hunting is definitely not a policing priority. It is not illegal to wear a red coat and ride a horse in a public place'.

SENSELESS

'Would not a man be by himself a month and go to bed before seven o'clock rather than mix with foxhunters who, having all day long tried in vain to break their necks, join at night in a second attempt upon their lives by drinking, and to express their mirth are louder in senseless sounds...than their barking and less troublesome companions.'

From The Fable of the Bees, *1705*
by Bernard de Mandeville

WHAT IS LIFE?

'That pleasure which the most enchants us,
Seems the soonest done;
What is life – with all it grants us –
But a hunting run?'

George Whyte-Melville, 1902

WHYTE-MELVILLE was an ex-Coldstream Guards officer who hunted with the Pytchley. He took up writing as a hobby. His best-selling novel *Market Harborough*, published in 1861 told the story of a country gent from the provinces who is shocked to discover that in the home counties hunting is all about speed. Whyte-Melville's twenty-eight sugary books have been described as 'one long campaign against drinking and gambling'. And to prove he was not just talk, he gave away much of his royalties to good causes, such as the provision of reading-rooms for stable-boys in hunting-quarters.

Whyte-Melville was a prissy fellow, impeccably turned out on the hunting field. He hated falling off and getting muddy. He loathed the steeplechasing of the fast hunts declaring that people who hurt their horses through speed were fools.

In 1878 Whyte-Melville became a famous hunting fatality when his horse fell in a ploughed field in the Vale of Pewsey. That night in the House of Commons one of his friends took aside Prime Minister Benjamin Disraeli, and whispered, 'Poor Whyte-Melville has been killed'.

Disraeli: 'How did that happen?'

Friend: 'Killed in the hunting field.'

Disraeli (solemnly): 'How very dramatic.'

• Whyte-Melville's marriage fell apart when his wife left him and remarried bigamously. The break-up affected him badly and he included his experiences in his 1874 novel *Uncle John*. Here Uncle John offers some excellent advice to a young man who is about to get married: 'Don't start with too exalted an idea of your goddess. She must come down from her pedestal sometimes. When she does not agree with you, don't be provoked with her because she is your wife, but listen to her courteously, though she is talking nonsense, as you would to any other lady. Above all, never attempt to reason with her as you would with a man.'

HUNTING GRACE

THE CRICKETER W. G. GRACE spent his winters riding to hounds. Despite his weight Grace was an acceptable horseman. In later years he retired from the saddle and took up beagling and otter hunting.

HOW TO HUNT IN 150 WORDS

'The fox is a very clever, cunning and pretty unpredictable wild animal, and contrary to what the antis will tell you, he starts with most of the high cards in his hand. To minimise this advantage is the objective of an MFH: a top class pack of hounds well managed in kennel, and well disciplined in the field; top class horses well managed in stable; efficient earth-stopping; good liaison with landowners, farmers and keepers; a good Field Master to control the field, and yet see they enjoy themselves; and finally the back up of the Hunt chairman and his committee, to see that the finance is there to do the job properly. If all the above is there, the fox can still disappear into thin air within a quarter of a mile. But at least you have attempted to see that it does not happen.'

Former Meynell huntsman Dermot Kelly, Foxhunting Companion, *Country Life Books, 1978*

STINKING RIDING

Gloriously chaotic scenes at the Army Staff College Drag Hunt's final meet of the 1896 season:

Tuesday, March 31st. Meet at Bannister's Farm. Alas! the last day of the season! To do honour to the occasion a field of forty-five mustered, all determined to ride hard. A perfect day, rather hot perhaps, with the smell of 'them stinking violets' in the air. A word of warning from the Secretary about a duck pond somewhere, and we are off. Forty yards in front was the first fence, beyond it the fateful pond. On the right, refusing galore; on the left – splash, and three sportsmen are in the pond. They were cadets, and the Easter Holiday is on, so they won't be required for a few days, and we left them there. Next comes the road, the landing boggy and trappy, but no grief. One horse made a fine double, clearing bank and bog first jump, and the opposite bank the next. The first whip has a fall early in the run, and is left with a horse without a bridle, or a bridle without a horse, we forget which. Graham's horse gave him a fall, and very nearly a second. De Tomkyn's slithered on to his nose, but got up cleverly. Burrowes arrived with a broken hat… After passing Handpost Farm the line swung right-handed down the hill west of Barkham Rectory. At this point a sporting pony in a trap tried to join the line. He got well on to the bank, but the cart wouldn't follow, and the driver got him back with difficulty. The line now swung to the left down a fine grass slope to Barkham Brook, Here there was much refusing, at one time nine horses fighting on the take off bank. One rider, not a S.C. man we hoped, at last dismounted in despair, and begged a spectator to 'ride the damned brute over'.

• Members of the Staff College Drag at the turn of the nineteenth century were known for the impressive array of injuries they could chalk up during the season. On the basis that hunting was training for war, a good splattering of blood and dislocated shoulders were de rigeur. Riders would carry on 'none the worse' for a broken collar bone, and the casualties of previous meets, known as 'The Cripples', would take up the rear in a dog cart. The hunt reports contained some good dry humour: 'February 3rd. 1896. Meet at Hayley Green Farm... One officer displayed considerable agility in getting back into the saddle after having been at one time in close proximity to his horse's ears. The horse fortunately had a very big head which prevented a total dissolution of partnership.'

• The social highpoint of the Staff College Drag's season was the Farmers' Dinner. According to reports, the wine was excellent, if on the cheap side: 'Our Secretary had provided us with an excellent fluid, which we had noticed him sampling about three times a week for the last month, "just to make sure it was all right, don't you know". It sparkled and fizzed like anything, was of a beautiful pale canary colour and the bottles were plastered with gold foil. The taste was a trifle peculiar, though not unpleasant'. The food also attracted attention, not least the vast array of puddings: 'The sweets were extremely popular. One gentleman... disposed of wine jelly, jam tarts, blanc-mange, fruit compote and Californian cream in a way that would have made the ordinary public schoolboy blush for shame.'

• Outsiders considered the Staff College Drag a frightful shower. A Hunt report contained the following conversation between a thrusting SC subaltern and a young lady whom he escorted into dinner while dining with friends in Berkshire.
She: 'I saw the Staff College drag today. I never saw such a rag-tag and bob-tailed assemblage in my life. Such poor riders, too.'
He : 'Yes. Not much of a lot, are they?'
She : 'No. Awful bounders!'
He : 'Yes – er, I'm one of them.'
Confusion and dismay on the part of the fair one.

• Today's Staff College Drag Hunt, based at the Royal Military Academy Sandhurst is a pale imitation of its derring do forebear. As usual, the whole thing has been bollocked up by health 'n safety. Members are ordered to read a 'Safety Code' and to sign a form absolving the Hunt of any responsibility should they injure themselves.

ANIMAL LOVERS

Cruellest attack by animal rights activists on a hunt happened in 2001 when forty-seven beagles were stolen from Wye College Beagles' kennels in Kent. Huntsman Dan Murphy arrived on the morning of 5 January to find the lodges empty. Later that morning the Animal Liberation Front claimed responsibility in an email to BBC Radio Kent.

Police made enquiries but the hounds had vanished. Only one was recovered, a stallion called Sextant, who was found in Bristol after a tip-off by a vet. During his time with the ALF, Sextant had been castrated and attempts had been made to remove his ear tattoo. An unemployed man called Julian Greensides pleaded guilty to theft by finding, but there was insufficient evidence to link him with the break-in. He got sixty hours community service after the judge referred to 'quasi-terrorist activity'.

None of Sextant's comrades resurfaced. It is thought that the ALF exterminated them having discovered that pack beagles make awful house pets. Sextant became a TV celebrity and attended Parliament Square demos to fight the hunting ban. He died in 2006 aged fourteen.

PRIVACY

PRINCE GEORGE, Duke of Cambridge (1819–1904), Commander in Chief of the British Army, was asked by a pushy mother what advice he could give her son, a recently gazetted Ensign. He replied that while out hunting the boy should keep an eye out for a haystack and to seek the privacy of said haystack should nature call.

> • The twentieth century hunting writer D. W. E. Brock MFH warned, 'The more you drink, even if it is only tea or water, before hunting, the more inconvenience you will have'. Referring to the problem of a male foxhunter being spotted having a pee by a lady subscriber, Brock added, 'If you must go behind a haystack and there isn't one, remember that if she's a lady she won't look, and if she isn't it doesn't matter anyway'.

CHILLING

At the end of each season the 1st Duke of Cleveland (1766–1842) published a chilling little pamphlet titled *Operations Of The Raby Pack*, a shaming exercise that included the minutiae of every case of over riding hounds. The Duke was fanatical about detail. His 1804–5 diaries record that he began hunting on 17 September and ended on 10 April, hunting ninety-one days in all, killing forty-nine foxes ('23 dogs, 10 bitches, 16 Doubtful') and earthing another twenty-four. He always fed hounds himself, never trusting a kennelman to do the job properly.

Cleveland kept hounds at Raby Castle for nearly fifty years hunting from south Yorkshire to Northumberland. In 1818 he successfully opposed plans for the first Stockton to Darlington railway on the grounds that it would cut across his coverts. The line was diverted.

The hunting journalist C. J. Apperley – 'Nimrod' – described how the Duke 'had a change of clothes kept well aired at all the principal inns within his hunt, to the nearest of which he always repaired when the sport was over; and putting himself into a chaise and four, ready dressed for the evening, a small field-piece at the lodge of his part announced his approach to the Castle; and by the time he arrived, dinner … was upon the table'.

• When hunting in the south of Raby country, the Duke of Cleveland lived at Newton House, Leeming, which boasted revolutionary kennels. A six inch deep channel led from the hounds' feeding room to their lodgings. This was filled with broth through which the hounds waded and afterwards licked their feet, thus using the healing properties of their tongues to cure any knicks or scratches incurred while hunting. The kennels were close to the house. When asked if the smell was unpleasant, Cleveland replied, 'We are too well bred to foxhunting to mind that, and a concord of sweet sounds from the kennels compensates for many unsavoury smells'.

• After a good day's sport it was the custom at Raby Castle to serve up a grilled fox tongue at dinner. Nobody ate it.

COLD

The worst yet season for hunting was 1844–5 when a harsh winter froze the ground solid for weeks. Hunts struggled to keep going and the Belvoir cancelled seventy-one days.

PRETTY GIRLS

WHILE trying to control an impatient field that was jostling hounds and huntman, Major Algy Burnaby, Master of the Quorn towards the end of the nineteenth century, was said to have addressed a crowd of ladies gathered near a covert side with the words: 'The pretty girls can stay with me – the ugly ones can go ahead'.

BUSES

ASKED WHY HE WAS RESIGNING the Mastership, an early twentieth century MFH of the Essex Foxhounds replied, 'The Mile End bus conductors head my foxes so often, I can stand it no longer'.

'WARE 'OLES, SAYS HE

SIR ARTHUR CONAN DOYLE
was fascinated by foxhunting.
Here he tells the fictitious story
of a hunting hero who
fell down a quarry.

A sportin' death! My word it was!
An' taken in a sportin' way.
Mind you, I wasn't there to see;
I only tell you what they say.

'E was a stranger to the 'Unt,
There weren't a person as 'e knew there;
But 'e could ride, that London gent –
'E sat 'is mare as if 'e grew there.

They seed the 'ounds upon the scent,
But found a fence across their track,
And 'ad to fly it; else it meant
A turnin' and a 'arkin' back.

'E was the foremost at the fence,
And as 'is mare just cleared the rail
He turned to them that rode be'ind,
For three was at 'is very tail.

''Ware 'oles!' says 'e, an' with the word,
Still sittin' easy on his mare, Down,
down 'e went, an' down an' down,
Into the quarry yawnin' there.
Some say it was two 'undred foot;
The bottom lay as black as ink.
I guess they 'ad some ugly dreams,
Who reined their 'orses on the brink.

'E'd only time for that one cry;
''Ware 'oles!' says 'e, an' saves all three.
There may be better deaths to die,
But that one's good enough for me.

For mind you, 'twas a sportin' end,
Upon a right good sportin' day;
They think a deal of 'im down 'ere,
That gent what came from London way.

'Ware Holes, by *Sir Arthur Conan Doyle*,
1898

MEATY STORIES

Advice for the new, young Master conducting his first puppy show:

'It is not a good thing to have your judges comes to blows in the ring over their mutual wife. Nor is it good to have judges with such entirely opposing views that they are still judging the doghounds at 9 o'clock at night.'

'If the young Master wants to make a good first impression, he should be wary of judges who relish telling meaty stories. Miss Spruce, who is 5ft of whale bone corset and long blue knickers, and who has walked four puppies a year for the past thirty, might not take kindly to the more way out antics of the actress and the bishop.'

'The young Master will be expected to say a few words of thanks to everybody, especially the puppy walkers. He should keep his speech, short, pithy and in one octave. If he should want to tell a funny story, I would suggest that he tries it on his kennelman first. Kennelmen are serious people, not much given to the frivolities of life. If the young Master gets a wintry smile, he is on to a real winner.'

'The puppy show tea is a high spot of the afternoon, but it should always be under cover – it is an established custom that it always rains during puppy show teas.'

'The young Master can go to great expense and call in a caterer who will produce a second rate tea at a first rate price. However, if he is going to make the grade as an MFH he should be able to do some crafty work amongst his female followers. No, not that sort of work.'

'The only certain advice I can give the young Master is that whatever drink the young Master may produce will disappear like dew… therefore I strongly advise concealing enough for a fighting whisky for himself afterwards. He will need it.'

'All in all, there is quite a lot of thought required in putting on a puppy show… over the years the young Master will perfect a system. I have quite a good one. I send my joint-Master a cable from the South of France and tell him to get on with the arrangements.'

From Arthur James, 'nom de plume of a respected amateur huntsman',
writing in the Foxhunting Companion, *Country Life Books, 1978*

LOVELINESS

The day after marrying young Boer War hero Sir John Milbanke, V.C. in December 1900, his wife Amelia was hunting with the Quorn. *The Field's* hunting correspondent 'Brooksby' commented, 'To marry a V.C. on a Thursday and lead the Quorn field on the Friday – is not this the height of desire of womanly loveliness?'

HUNTERS' GRAVEYARD

BACK IN THE EARLY 1900s The Meath and other hunts in Dublin country were attended by gangs of labourers known as 'wreckers'. These men would stand by in case a horse disappeared into one of the deep waterlogged boundary ditches for which that part of Ireland was famous. Armed with ropes and spades, they extricated any unfortunate animals in return for a sovereign.

The wreckers were entirely mercenary. They were reputed to encourage visitors to ride at treacherous fences – only to discover a deep hole behind. Sometimes they would push a horse back into a ditch as he teetered on the brink. They would do anything so long as it earned them money. The wreckers were particularly numerous whenever the Ward Union staghounds met at Bush Farm, Fairyhouse, known as a the Hunters' Graveyard. Most of the fences were considered unjumpable.

FORGOTTEN HUNTING METROPOLIS

England's forgotten hunting metropolis is Royal Leamington Spa, Warwickshire.

THESE DAYS LEAMINGTON is an unexciting dormitory town to Warwick, notable for its student accommodation. Back in the early nineteenth century it was bursting into life as a glorious hunting centre, second only to Melton Mowbray. At its sporting height the town boasted twenty-two mews with stabling for hundreds of hunters.

Within twenty-five miles of Leamington there were more than 140 coverts for the North Warwickshire, the Drake's, Pytchley and Atherstone hounds. By 1820 the Leamington hunting set were firmly entrenched. A writer described the town as 'half-hunting and half-water drinking and waltzing'. The Warwickshire Hunt Ball was the social event of the year. There were endless hunt dinners.

Many Leamingtonites stayed on after the hunting season to take the waters and promenade through the town's pretty streets. Somebody wrote that the word 'season' was meaningless in Leamington because there were parties all year round. As in Melton, clubs sprung up in houses around the town, notably The Oyster Club and Copp's, 'fitted up at enormous expensive' by Viscount Eastnor.

Before the railways arrived in the mid-nineteenth century there were dozens of regular coaches from Leamington to every major town in southern England. In 1827 the Duke and Duchess of St Albans made Leamington their winter home so that he could hunt with the Warwickshire and she could entertain in grand style. Much was made of a remark that the Duchess reputedly uttered to her husband: 'Well your Grace, if you can find amusement in the field for the day, I will endeavour to provide for the evening, and we will see if we cannot make Leamington as pleasant in winter as it is gay in summer'.

By the 1850s the town was losing its appeal. The adjacent countryside was brilliant for hunting but it was flat and dull, not at all romantic or picturesque; nothing like Leicestershire. In winter the social life was limited and the town could offer little more than hunting, and that wasn't doing very well. In 1858 the Warwickshire bagged only 84 foxes in 123 days. Nor was the field particularly distinguished. One commentator remarked that people who hunted out of Leamington tended to be rather common. There were too many commuter-hunters from London who 'did not, as a rule, conduce to the peace of mind of the Master or the enjoyment of the sport by those who hunted for hunting's sake'.

• A magazine called *The Sunbeam* offered a good description of the Leamington hunting scene in 1838: 'In the hunting season, the huge stone hotels of Leamington assume the character of vast hunting lodges. Early in the morning the large quadrangular courtyards at Copp's or the Regent, surrounded by solid stone stabling, having loose boxes and all the requisite conveniences for hunters, are alive with the movements of grooms and stable boys. High bred silky hunters are next led forth, and light compact servants, in suitable livery slowly depart with them for the covert, riding some and leading others. At a later hour nimble valets are flying about the passages of the hotel, bearing on their arms buckskin breeches and gloves, newly cleaned, top-boots, the tops white as milk; and polished spurs... Seats at the breakfast table are gradually occupied by fresh looking gentlemen, in loose morning gowns and slippers, all attired for the hunt, excepting coats and boots, who deliberately partake of cold pheasant or mincemeats, dry toast and coffee, make a few quaint observations to each other on the nature of the weather and its aptness for the scent, and on rising some cast themselves into spacious elbow-chairs by the cheerful hearth at each end of the breakfast hall, while others disappear as quietly as they entered. At ten o'clock the scene without becomes animated. Covert hackneys are led to the entrance, and gentlemen in scarlet coats, bright coloured cravats, buckskin breeches and gloves, top-boots, and having heavy, long-lashed hunting whips are seen mounting and cantering off to the field, while the bright eyes of ladies look forth from casements, and now and then, some gallant hunter will pass with majestic steps beneath the windows, the easy yet graceful position of his rider indicating to the practised eye the finished sportsman. The streets between their slabbed side walks and stately houses present a gay procession during the departure for the hunt, and then in contrast, seem as silent and lifeless as the aisles of a church. Toward evening straggling parties are seen threading the streets in various plight, showing symptoms of the run; dismount at the hotels; and their horses, drooping their heads, with hollow flank and weary carriage, are led to the stables. Then succeeds the savoury dinner, the quickening champagne, the heart-restoring port. Cheeks that were pale with hard riding, now rival the ruddy hue of the hunting coat, and conviviality reigns over the board.'

PAINS

'I don't ride and have no empathy with horses. But I do approve of hunting for ecological reasons. Hunt saboteurs are stupid, fanatical pains in the backside who are immune to logic.'

Thriller writer Frederick Forsyth, 1995

LAST RANT

HOUND BREEDING can obsess foxhunters to the very end. Will Smith, huntsman with the Brocklesby, died after a fall in April 1845. Referring to his favourite hound, his last words as he lay in the field were: 'Mind my successor never loses sight of Ranter or his blood'.

CARPING

'Masters frequently debate, in their secret conclaves, whether there is any way of abolishing the Field. They are confident that hunting would be removed above carping criticism if no one hunted.'

Humourist Frederick Watson, Hunting Pie, *1931*

RAMBLE

HOUNDS HAVING LOST THE SCENT, the MFH stopped to ask a yokel if he had seen the fox. The yokel rambled on and on about how he had indeed the seen the fox, and how it had gone this way and that way and this way again, etc. etc.

'And was he as talkative as you?' asked the Master with scowl.

'Yes, sir, 'e woz. 'E asks me whose hounds be after 'im. I says yours be, sir. 'Ah', sez the fox. Then no need to 'urry.'

SAFE

MARGOT ASQUITH, wife of the Liberal Prime Minister Henry Asquith, a steady but unexciting man, named her hunter…Henry. 'I called him that,' she explained, 'because he is so safe'.

URBAN FOX

The last proper fox hunt in what is now central London was conducted by the Old Berkeley in around 1795 under the command of their longstanding huntsman Tom Oldaker. The Old Berkeley's country spread all the way from west London to Gloucestershire. One of Oldaker's final runs featured a find in Scratch Wood, a covert on the edge of Wormwood Scrubs. The pack chased the fox as far as Kensington Gardens where it was lost in rough ground.

> • Until the eighteenth century, the Old Berkeley staghounds were kenneled at Charing Cross. They hunted in Gray's Inn Fields and Islington.

VILEST SLAVE

Least fondly remembered English huntsmen was an oaf called Jack Ware, who worked for the Charlton Hunt in the 1720s. The Charlton's annals described Ware as 'most indifferent' and a 'vilest slave'. He was hopeless in the field and his hounds were riddled with mange. He lost his job after getting blind drunk, taking the pack out on his own, and allowing them to kill fourteen sheep in an afternoon.

SCREAMS

MOST ENTERTAINING finish in the history of foxhunting happened on Easter Monday, 1803, when John Corbet's hounds of the Warwickshire Hunt ended up in Lady Hertford's ornamental dairy at Ragley Hall. This exquisite moment was captured in a ditty penned by a member of the Hunt:

'The pack, heedless of the damsels' screams,
First ate the fox – then drank the cream.'

Lady Hertford was described as 'tall, handsome, and elegant but a little portly'. She married the 2nd Marquis of Hertford in 1776 when she was just sixteen and he was thirty-four. She eventually tired of Hertford and at the age of forty-eight took up with the Prince Regent – two years her junior – with whom she conducted an affair for twelve years.

CARDIGAN NOT A JUMPER

The 7th Earl of Cardigan, 'hero' of the Light Brigade cock-up in the Crimea, died after falling from his horse while attempting to take a fence while hunting near his Northamptonshire seat Deene Park on 28 March 1868. He was seventy. Nobody knows exactly what happened, but his horse came home without him. A search party found the injured peer in a field. He is believed to have had a stroke.

THE COW THAT HUNTED

WHILE A HUMBLE *Sunday Express* racing correspondent, and several years before achieving fame as a thriller writer, former professional jockey Dick Francis wrote a piece for a 1960 book called *In Praise Of Hunting*. Francis, who first went hunting aged seven, described how his grandfather was addicted to the sport:

'When he was a young man, at the end of the last century, my grandfather Willie Francis was a top amateur steeplechase jockey. He spent every non-racing day out with hounds during the hunting season, as, though he was supposed to be farming, he considered horses the only important thing in life. It so happened that he was cantering down a lane at the head of the field...when out of an open gate a large cow strolled unconcernedly straight acrosss the middle of the lane twenty yards ahead of him. Willie...clicked his tongue, dug in his heels, and he and his horse sailed clean over the cow. This sight so shook the following Hunt that the story was told to me in my boyhood by at least ten people who had witnessed it. Willie was no fool: he was an excellent jockey out hunting on a top-class 'chaser, and the only difference between the cow and Becher's was that the cow was moving!'

• Francis had entertaining views on that accursed subject of finding the right hunter: 'It is no use expecting too much loyalty from a horse. Should one be unlucky enough to fall off out hunting, one's horse will heartlessly gallop away after the hounds leaving his bruised and dishevelled rider to trudge for miles in his wake. There are two exceptions to the dump 'em and leave 'em rule. First, very common horses (who have less love of hunting than better bred ones) will not go more than a field or two before they get their heads down to the grass. Grub, not glory, for this lot. Secondly, those horses whose riders constantly fall off (perish the thought!) get into the habit of expecting it as a normal part of a day's hunting. They will often stand patiently by, munching, waiting to be remounted. But here again, they are likely to be a bit common, as so helpless a rider would scarcely aspire to a blood horse. One excitable show-jumper I used to ride was so stirred up by the smells, noises and sights of a show that he pranced and fussed himself into a sweat every time he was due to jump. The result was too often a sad trail of faults. One season's hunting had failed to cure him, so the following winter I took him out only on bad scenting days or to districts almost devoid of foxes, and stationed him at distant edges of coverts where little was likely to happen. We spent hours waiting about, and it bored us both stiff: but no horse behaved more quietly at the shows the next summer.'

(Copyright Dick Francis 1960)

From In Praise of Hunting, *Hollis & Carter, 1960*

THE GREAT TIDE OF SPECIES

'ONLY ONE KIND OF HORSE gets the most out of being a horse and that is the hunter. Alone among domesticated animals the hunter has the chance to run with the herd – fit, well fed and carefree – over country cleared of his natural predators. No equine joy matches that of running side by side with other horses, immersed in the great tide of species and excited by the baying of hounds.'

From On Hunting, *by Roger Scruton, foxhunting philosopher, Yellow Jersey Press, 1998*

BUCKETS OF BLOOD

Worst lost of equine life on a hunting field happened on 16 January 1845, following a savagely quick chase with the Warwickshire Hunt. In what became known as the Hillmorton Run, thirteen horses died, most of them back at stables thanks to the practice of bleeding which was supposed to revive tired horses. A member of the hunt staff recalled: 'I never saw such a sight as the stableyard at Dunchurch – buckets of blood on all sides'.

VERBOTEN

Thanks to Hitler, hunting with hounds is verboten in Germany. The Fuhrer, a vegetarian and all round fluffy bunny man, was the pioneer of hunting bans. He viewed German fox-hunters as aristocratic, effete and probably Anglophile.

On 3 July 1934, on the orders of Hermann Goering, hunting was banned throughout Germany on the grounds that pursuing animals with hounds was 'unsporting'. The law was adopted under a moral code called Waidgerechtigkeit – sporting justice. Goering also argued that hunting was helping to spread rabies from eastern Europe.

In 1939, the ban was extended to cover Austria after Germany's annexation of the country. Much to Hitler's delight, the ban provoked fury amongst the aristocracy who for centuries had hunted foxes, boar and deer. It can be said that the Nazis and New Labour shared similar reasons for wanting to ban hunting: both had monstrous chips on their shoulders and erroneously equated hunting with toffs.

Goering was a passionate shot who had appointed himself Reichsjaegermeister, which roughly translates as Shoot Captain of the Reich. He enjoyed stalking but hated the idea of hunting with hounds. During their tenure, the Nazis gave animals more protection than any other country in the world. There was a strangely ethical side to the reforms. They wanted to see a clean kill and felt that it was wrong to cause unnecessary suffering. Thus their laws banned field sports that used animals to kill. Moreover, the hunting ban seems to have been part of a larger plan to give every German hunter his own reserve on which to shoot once lands such as Russia had been conquered.

Hunting with hounds is still banned in Germany. Since 1934 foxes have been killed only by guns, although terriers and dachshunds are used to drive them out when they go to ground. Bloodhounds are used to track down wounded game but not to kill.

• Goering's fashion sense has also stood the test of time. Most of Germany's 330,000 registered hunters still dress in the green loden hunting garb and feathered hat that he wore as Reichsjaegermeister.

STRANGE

'It is very strange, and very melancholy, that the paucity of human pleasures should persuade us ever to call hunting one of them.' Eighteenth century essayist Dr. Samuel Johnson, who followed hounds a few times but never really enjoyed it.

PECULIAR PRIVILEGE

'THE FIELD IS A MOST AGREEABLE COFFEE HOUSE, and there is more real society to be met with there than in any other situation in life. It links all classes together, from the Peer to the peasant'. John Hawkes, Meynellian Science, 1808

Hawkes' book was a tribute to Quorn Master Hugo Meynell. Hawkes was a country gent who rode with the Warwickshire Hunt. An obituarist described him as 'the best gentleman rider in the country.' A story is told of how Hawkes rode a steeplechase for George IV. Hawkes lost whereupon the king asked him if his spurs were the best he had. When Hawkes said, 'Yes,' the king handed over his own pair of spurs hoping that they might help Hawkes to win next time. Hawkes, who died in 1834 at his country seat outside Cannock, Staffordshire, had a quick wit. When asked by someone he met at the races how he liked a particular horse, he replied, 'I like very few horses, very few women and damned few men'.

> • Hawkes hated 'whippers-in ' who were 'too apt to think of their own importance' and consequently made too much noise when calling hounds. 'Whippers-in should turn hounds quietly, and not call after them in a noisy disagreeable manner. When hounds are going to cry, they should be encouraged in a pleasant way, not driven and rated, as if discord was a necessary ingredient in the sport'.

SOME SORT OF DRUG

'THERE IS LITTLE DOUBT THAT PEOPLE will do things when they are hunting that they would never consider in cold blood. It is almost as if they have had a shot of some sort of drug that dulls their normal fears – for who would think of jumping an iron gate for the fun of it except perhaps the very young, or may I be permitted to say, the foolhardy?'

From Foxhunting, *by the Duke of Beaufort, David & Charles, 1988*

VELVETEEN AT WAR WITH SCARLET

THE VICTORIAN OBSESSION for stuffing anything that moved became the target for *Baily's Magazine of Sports and Pastimes* which in 1861 carried this rant on the 'evils' of stuffed foxes:

'Greatly to the detriment of our sport, numbers of foxes are destroyed annually for this purpose to be exhibited in private collections or paraded before the public eye in the shop windows of saddlers, poulterers and others as an intimation of the sporting propensities of the exhibitors. And then the stuffers, one or two of whom are to be found in most towns, carry on an illicit trade in fox skins of which they have no

scruple in boasting. These foxes are purchased from poachers at sums varying from five to ten shillings each. A fox to these men is as good as a brace of pheasants, and so long as there are receivers there will be fox stealers.'

Baily's concluded with a plea to owners of shooting estates, particularly in Norfolk, who were partial to decorating their houses with stuffed foxes: 'There is no necessity for velveteen to be at war with scarlet because their tastes and pursuits differ. We don't envy you the use of your dog and gun or your heavy bag of game, but don't from too selfish considerations bag our fox too …'

THE HUNTING EXPRESS

A part from a bit of soldiering in his youth and a stint as an MP, Henry Somerset, 8th Duke of Beaufort, spent his life hunting. The Duke conceived the Badminton Library series of sporting books – named after his Gloucestershire seat – which began publication in 1885 with a volume titled Hunting. Something of a closet train spotter, His Grace penned the following piece, containing valuable advice for the Victorian foxhunter intending to hunt from London by train:

'If you do not mind taking your pleasure somewhat laboriously, you may get plenty of hunting without ever passing a winter's night away from your London home. There is no reason why you should not enjoy your gallop with the Old Berkshire, the South Berkshire, the Bicester, the Heythrop, the Duke of Grafton's, and Mr Selby-Lowndes', nay, no reason why you should not penetrate into the very Shires themselves. By leaving King's Cross at 7.45 you can reach Grantham at 10.35, and a train from the same station starting half an hour earlier will land you at Melton at 10.32. Leaving Euston at 7.30 you reach Rugby at 9.34; leaving St Pancras at 8.10, you reach Market Harboro' at 10.44. In short, if not sorrow, it is labour. It is not only the early rising; though that alone, on a dark winter's morning when the water is of dubious warmth, and the fire probably will do nothing but smoke, in sullen protest against its unseasonable lighting, does indeed entail something of a struggle on this poor frail human flesh. To dress by candlelight is never an enlivening process, and when the dress is such as men go a-hunting in, it is often little short of misery. To button those knee-buttons, and tie those natty little bows below them, by the uncertain light of a candle, and with blue fingers senseless with cold – ah! my friend, nate mecum Consule Manlio – must one not be very fond of the game… But these are, after all, mere sensual sorrows. The man who would grudge to give his morning sleep for a gallop over the grass is unworthy the name of a sportsman and a Briton!

'The question remains, in what style will he elect to take his hunting ? Will he keep his horses in London and carry them backwards and forwards with him by rail, or will he settle them in quarters at the town most convenient to the fixtures of the pack with which he intends to hunt? Much can be said for either plan, much against it. Let us take the former first. The advantages of this course are clear. His horses will be under his own eye, and he will be able to vary his country at his pleasure. On the other hand, he will have to make an earlier start ; unless, of course, he sends his hunter down with a groom, and himself follows with a hack by a later train, or even sends horse and man down the day before; both of which plans will obviously swell the expenses not a

THE KEEN FOXHUNTER'S MISCELLANY

little… What does concern the horse is the railway journey. On some horses a journey by rail has no more effect than on some human beings. On others it has a most injurious effect, both on their nerves and their temper. It is almost inevitable, too, from the confined space in which the horse is necessarily penned during the journey, that a certain stiffness will be visible when released at its end. If, however, he is a sedate and even-tempered beast, this will pass away soon enough when he breathes the fresh air and stretches his limbs; and if he is not that, he had better be got rid of quickly, for he will be of little use in this game.

'Then, there is the return journey. Never, if it can possibly be avoided, should you ride your horse straight from the field to the nearest station, and have him put just as he is into a box to catch the first train home. He should first be roughly dressed down, his legs and feet dry-rubbed and bandaged, and his inner horse mildly refreshed with a mouthful of gruel.'

• The railways brought foxhunting into a golden age from 1850. Businessmen no longer needed to buy country houses with stables in order to hunt and nationally the number of packs grew from 99 in 1850 to 137 in 1877. Fields in the Midlands regularly reached three hundred. You could leave Euston Station in London at 6.30am to hunt with the Pytchley and return to London the same night. By 1854 twenty-four packs could be hunted from London in a day. A 'special' hunting train, with stabling trucks, could be made up at most stations at short notice. And to help you plan your season there was a new publication called *The Foxhunter's Guide*, listing meets and their distance from railway stations. Not everybody liked the railways. Lord Redesdale resigned as Master of the Heythrop in 1853 in protest at the track going through his country. And hunting writer Surtees complained that the trains made it too easy for the gentry to leave their homes for London and thus abandon healthy hunting for the wicked pleasures of the city.

UNLUCKY BIRD

MR RICHARD MORRIS, a whipper-in with
the Puckeridge during the 1850s, is said to have
killed a flying woodcock with his whip.

LEGLESS

TOWARDS the end of the eighteenth century the Quorn employed a
whipper-in called Joseph 'cork-legged' Jones on account of his artificial
leg. Jones was a great rider and a great drinker. He managed well until he got
drunk, when he would awake unable to remember where he had left his leg
overnight. Inconvenient on a hunting day.

BULLS UP

POSSIBLY THE ONLY HUNTSMAN to have deliberately hunted and
killed a bull was Bob Ward, who hunted a pack called Mr Wood's Harriers
during the 1830s. Known as 'Ubiquity Bob', Ward was an exceptional
huntsman who occasionally became carried away by his own enthusiasm. The
bull hunting escapade, during which he turned his hounds on a miserable
creature that was doing little more dangerous than munch grass, was but a
glitch in an otherwise glittering career.

> • Mr Wood's Harriers hunted from the once charming village of
> Newton-le-Willows, Lancashire, since swallowed up by Merseyside.

OOTY FOX

THE ONLY SURVIVING fox hunt east of Suez is The Ooty Hunt Club, founded in 1835 by British residents of Ootacamund, a hill station in the south Indian state of Tamil Nadu. Today the Ooty's membership is ninety-five percent Indian but as you charge across the rolling Home Downs dressed in scarlet coats with green collar, you could well be in England, perhaps the New Forest. The giveaway is that many of the riders are in turbans.

The hunt was formed by the 74th Highland Regiment to chase sambur deer, bison, wild boar and the odd tiger. These days the quarry is jackal.

The Ooty has hunted every year since its foundation, with a pause in 1857 for the Indian Mutiny. There is no stirrup cup at meets, only tea served by liveried bearers . There are fines for anyone who refer to hounds as 'dogs' or for those who fall off during the day. The hunt's HQ is the Oootacamund Club, a dusty relic of the raj, which still boasts a portrait of a young Queen Elizabeth in the bridge room. The hunt seems concentrates on being seen to do the right thing and to have a jolly good ride rather than actually hunt. The Ooty hounds have not caught a jackal since 1976.

DAMNED

The Berwickshire, the oldest hunt in Scotland, is reputed to have the worst scenting country in the British Isles. It is so bad that, according to the fictional Jorrocks, the worst insult you can hurl at a foxhunter is: 'May you be damned to hunt in Berwickshire for the rest of your days'.

DASTARDLY TRAITORS

A SHORTAGE OF ENGLISH FOXES towards the end of the eighteenth century led hunts to import their quarry from the Continent. Throughout the nineteenth century thousands of mainly French and Dutch 'bagged' foxes were sold at London's Leadenhall Market giving these miserable creatures the nickname 'Leadenhallers' or 'bagmen'. They were shipped from Rotterdam in small rabbit cages aboard cattle ships and were big business for game dealers. For the first time an inedible animal had become a consumable product.

Although they guaranteed sport on what might otherwise be a blank day, bagged foxes are hopeless to hunt. If you leave a fox in a bag for several hours it will carry so much scent that hounds find it easy to track. Also, it will emerge from its bag so stiff after being tied up that it will often collapse after a short run. If it does manage to run, because it doesn't know the country, and still thinks it's in Holland, it will tear across open fields making it easy for the huntsman to spot – an English fox will use local knowledge to scuttle half-hidden along ditches and streams.

Captive foxes were thought to spoil hounds. French foxes, dug out by peasants in the countryside outside Paris, were considered to be particularly degenerate since they brought mange with them. The hunting author Surtees called the bagged fox 'a short running dastardly traitor'. He let down the field because he wouldn't run properly. He refused to play the game and that simply wasn't on.

But thanks to the disastrously short supply of native English foxes by the end of the nineteenth century, the bagman had become a necessity. Foxhunting was at the peak of its popularity. The railways had opened the countryside up townies and the sport was being taken up by the rising middle classes keen to improve their social standing.

Charles Richardson, hunting editor of *The Field*, blamed the fox shortage on gamekeepers indulging in wanton vulpicide thanks to the new fashion for large scale pheasant shooting. 'In many districts foxes have disappeared in wholesale fashion, and the hunting has become little more than a farce.'

Cunning landowners would order their keepers to slaughter all the native foxes and then, in order to keep appearances, would grandiosely invite the hunt onto their land having secretly released a bagged animal which they knew would be caught immediately and was too useless to kill their pheasants. Richardson recalled a meet where hounds drew three foxes, all of which had obviously come on the coach from London. 'The first one had a shower of chaff on his coat from the bedding in the box in which he had travelled from Leadenhall; the second and third had the remains of labels around their necks.'

• The largest Georgian game dealer specialising in bagged foxes was Philip Castang, whose premises were near the Tower of London. His stock came from as far away as Russia. Castang boasted in a newspaper advertisement: 'Supplier of foxes to Her Majesty the Queen during the hunting season'. His biggest order came from an unnamed Master of Foxhounds in a south of England hunt which had run out of indigenous foxes. In three weeks Castang used his contacts to gather not less than 150 bagmen from Holland, France, Germany and Scotland. Once the creatures had arrived in London, Castang packed them into crates on six coaches and sent them off to his client. The price was extortionate – small ones 12s/6d (62½p) and large ones 15/- (75 p).

• An early nineteenth century Master called George Templer, of Stover, South Devon, ran a pack of dwarf foxhounds specially for hunting bagged foxes. The hounds, just nineteen inches tall, were trained not to kill and became known as the 'Let 'em alones'. They were never allowed blood, except when invited to a meet out of their country. To keep the pack amused, Templer kept a supply of twenty bought foxes in coops behind his stables. One of his tame foxes, called The Bold Dragoon, was turned down (bagged foxes are 'turned down', never 'let out') no less than thirty-six times. According to Templer, he 'never failed to enjoy his freshly-killed rabbit on his return from being hunted'. One can only imagine that on the thirty-seventh time, he was not so lucky. Templer was a wild eccentric who trained a monkey to ride a hunter. The monkey quite enjoyed itself and would accompany Templer to meets. Unfortunately, the creature met its end when struck by a swinging gate. Whenever he hunted in Dorset, Templer took two extra horses, one bearing the stable cat, and the other his favourite tame fox called Latitat. Templer also kept a tame jackal (not taught to hunt).

• Tom Hills, a seventeenth century Old Surrey huntsman, was returning home one evening with a fox he had bought in Leadenhall Market when he was stopped by a highwayman on Streatham Common. Hills told the blackguard to help himself to the pocket which contained the fox. Hills escaped leaving the highwayman nursing severely bitten fingers.

• The Master of Foxhounds Association outlawed the hunting of bagged foxes upon its formation in 1881.

BEAUFORT'S CORRECT FORM

THE 10TH DUKE OF BEAUFORT (1900–1984), greatest hunting Beaufort of 'em all and Master for a record sixty-two years, considered it vulgar to refer to hunting 'pink'. The word pink was used by ignorant journalists, who had got it into their heads (incorrectly) that it had something to do with a tailor called Thomas Pink. According to Beaufort the hunting coat was always 'red', though 'scarlet' was acceptable if you were Army.

Beaufort was a stickler for correct form. He decreed that one should always refer to a hunting 'tie' and never a 'stock'. 'To me a stock is part of a gun', the Duke complained. 'Or something that is used to make soup'. His contribution to foxhunting was so great that he was known to all as 'Master', including his wife. As Marquess of Worcester he was given his own pack of harriers at the age of eleven. When commissioned into the Royal Horse Guards, he wangled special leave allowing him to hunt two days a week.

Beaufort was terrifyingly knowledgeable about everything from kennel management to the correct position of a tie-pin. He was a fine breeder and judge of hounds and his proudest possessions were his old established female lines.

Here is 'Master's' list of what you should have in your pockets on a hunting day:

1. A handkerchief. A clean white one if hunting with a Moorland pack, as it will show up when you wave it up to show which way the fox has gone

2. A pocket knife with a spike to make holes in leather in case of a repair.

3. Binder twine for tying up gates, repairs to saddlery etc.

4. Hair pins and spare hair nets (for ladies.)

5. Sustenance, but beware that ribs have been broken by coming into contact with a steel flask in a breast pocket.

6. Your name and address on a card in case you are knocked out.*

From Foxhunting, *by the Duke of Beaufort,* David & Charles, 1988

---

* Some Beaufort subscribers used to carry a card bearing the words: 'If found injured, on no account take me to Cheltenham General.'

• Until the early 1760s the Dukes of Beaufort hunted stags. The story goes that after that a disappointing morning stag hunting, the 5th duke drew Silk Wood (now part of Westonbirt Arboretum) in the hope of finding a fox. A brilliant days' sport resulted…and so began the Duke of Beaufort's Fox Hounds.

• The 10th Duke of Beaufort was determined to bring foxhunting to the masses. In 1962 he helped start the Banwen Valley Hunt in West Glamorgan, a Welsh miner's pack, whose kennels were established in the lamp room of the colliery in Branwen.

• The 10th Duke of Beaufort died in February 1984. On Christmas night 1984 his grave was desecrated by animal rights activists who sprayed anti-hunting slogans around Badmington churchyard.

• The Beaufort is one of the few remaining private packs in England, although it is mostly financed by subscription.

OLDEST

Oldest hunt in England is the Bilsdale, in Yorkshire, founded in 1668 by George Villiers, 2nd Duke of Buckingham, the debauched playboy and wit about whom was written the nursery rhyme 'Georgie Porgie pudding and pie, kissed the girls and made them cry'. In April 1687, after flogging his horse to exhaustion in the course of a day's hunting, Villiers fell off, went to sleep in the wet grass and caught a chill. He was taken to the house of a tenant where he died.

• The South and West Wilts also lays claim to being the oldest hunt in England but is probably just pipped by the Bilsdale. The packs' rivalry is not helped by the Master of Fox Hounds Association. Ever tactful and perhaps keen to avoid a row, the MFHA states on two separate web pages that each pack is the oldest in England.

PRIORITIES

BRITAIN'S FIRST PRIME MINISTER Sir Robert Walpole was obsessed by hunting both fox and hare. Any spare time would find him at his Norfolk family seat Houghton Hall where he hunted frequently throughout the 1720s and 1730s. Walpole built up huge debts in pursuit of his life as a country gent. A letter from his huntsman or gamekeeper always took precedence over a political dispatch.

HUNTING MAD

MOST UNUSUAL PACK OF HOUNDS in England were the harriers at Ticehurst House Hospital, a mental institution in Sussex.

During Victorian times Ticehurst became the most famous upper class loony bin in Britain. The aristocracy and gentry found it a convenient place to dump their erring relations, whether they be girls who threatened to marry beneath them (and were therefore obviously insane) or boys who were thought to be spending too much time masturbating (and therefore obviously insane). Inmates were subjected to all sorts of treatments from electric shock therapy to the application of sulphur to the foreskin.

But not all was gloom at Ticehurst. During the summer there was croquet, archery, and bowls.

And in winter there was hunting.

The Ticehurst House Harriers, founded in the 1820s, were intended to provide patients with much-needed exercise. But by the end of the nineteenth century hounds seldom left kennels. A member of staff lamented, 'Unless a man has a liking for hunting, it is most difficult to create any enthusiasm for it'. Ticehurst patients were too rich, well bred and lazy to involve themselves in strenuous exercise. 'We find it impossible to induce the class we have to deal with to undertake anything in the way of manual labour against their will'.

• Ticehurst continues to operate as a private mental hospital owned by the Priory Group. The hounds are long gone.

POETIC PONG

The writer Hartley Coleridge (1796–1849) spent his life living in the shadow of his famous father, the poet Samuel Taylor Coleridge. But Hartley did come up with one memorable line. Referring to hounds' fondness for the scent of fox, he wrote, 'What seems to us merely a disagreeable smell, is perhaps to their canine organs a most beautiful poem'.

A critic replied, 'Beautiful as it may be, both masters and huntsmen have so far been unable to discover, even approximately, the laws on which that poem is constructed…'.

MAGNIFIQUE

AFTER THE CHARGE OF THE LIGHT BRIGADE and the slaughter of 478 English cavalrymen, the French General Pierre Bosquet remarked 'C'est magnifique mais ce n'est pas la guerre: c'est de la folie'. He confided to fellow officers that the attack had been more like a day's fox-hunting in England. Meanwhile, Lord George Paget, in command of the 4th Light Dragoons, seemed to be under the impression that he was on a day out with the Pytchley. Paget remarked that the charge against the Russian guns at Balaclava was like 'the finest run in Leicestershire'. A fellow officer even yelled 'tally-ho' as his hunter leapt over the Russian battery.

• Proving that foxhunting is as close to war as you will get, Victorian military historian Alexander Kinglake described how Colonel Lacy Yea, legendary commander of the 7th Fusiliers at the Battle of Alma, a man of 'fiery, violent nature', used his hunting skills to surprise the enemy. 'Lacy Yea had been used in early days to ride to hounds in the stiffest of hunting countries. To him the left bank of the Alma, crowned with Russian troops, was like the wayside activity which often enough in his boy-hood had threatened to wall back and keep him down in the depths of a Somersetshire lane whilst the hounds were running high up in the field some ten or fifteen feet above. His practised eye soon showed him a break in the scarped face of the bank, and then shouting out to his people, "Never mind forming! Come on, men! Come on anyhow", he put his cob to the task and quickly gained the top. On either side of him men of his regiment quickly climbed up, and in such numbers that the Russian skirmishers who had been lining it fell back upon their battalions'.

IMAGE LIFT

The description of hunting as 'the image of war without its guilt' is often attributed to Jorrocks, the fictitious MFH in Robert Surtees' 1843 novel *Handley Cross*. In fact, Surtees lifted this line from the poet William Somerville who used it 108 years earlier in his epic 1735 hunting poem *The Chase:*

> While crowded theatres, too fondly proud
> Of their exotic minstrels, and shrill pipes.
> The price of manhood, hail thee with a song
> And airs soft warbling: my hoarse sounding horn
> Invites thee to the chase, the sport of kings;
> Image of war, without its guilt.

FASHION NOTE

Important hunting terminology:

Breeches split, but hounds divide.

DON'T MENTION THE DOG

THE FIRST PACK IN AUSTRALIA was the Sydney Hunt Club which hunted the country outside the capital in the 1830s. They chased dingos.

Members of the club were subject to strict rules, the most bizarre of which was that they should never refer to their quarry as dogs. At a dinner in 1836 it was proposed that members should always talk about the 'Australian fox'. To mention the word dog would result in a fine of half a crown.

By the 1850s the Sydney had no need for such rules as they were now importing English foxes into Australia. The creatures bred and by the 1890s there was such a serious fox problem in Victoria that the government gave a bounty on pelts.

The successor to the Sydney is the Goulburn Valley Fox Hounds which today hunts foxes along the lower Goulburn River area. The hounds are Kerry Beagles imported from Ireland. Their lighter frames make them suited to hunting the thick forest area along the river.

There are a total of thirteen hunts in Australia comprising around 1000 members.

FOX FIX

'The mark of a free society is one where you are free
to snort a line of cocaine while you
wait for a fox to break cover.'

Playwright Sir Tom Stoppard

GLIMPSES OF CHARLIE

Today's answer to the great Victorian hunting writers Surtees and Nimrod is Old Etonian Charles Moore who writes a sadly all too occasional hunting column in the *Spectator* magazine.

Journalistic heavyweight Moore, former editor of the *Daily Telegraph*, writes his column with unabashed enthusiasm. Mindful of the wretched ban, he avoids too much politics, as favoured by lesser hunting commentators, and concentrates instead on the poetic, glorious side to the chase. This is in contrast to most hunting writers who are more concerned about making the sport look 'respectable' to outsiders rather than relishing the action in the field.

Moore explains: 'Anyone who loves hunting must do his best to stay out till the end so that he experiences every gradation of the day – its early nerves, its settled middle period, its gentle decline – or, sometimes, its late excitement as the falling temperature improves the scent and we find a travelling fox at dusk'.

Here is one of Moore's contributions, from the January 2003 *Spectator*:

'The fox is often called Charlie (after Charles James Fox), and that is a good sign, because you don't give a name to the rats you poison or the cockroaches you smoke out. One of the pleasures of the hunt is the snatched glimpses of Charlie and the instances of his sagacity. I have seen him try to creep past us as hounds sniff uncertainly round a farmyard. I have seen him trot unconcerned under our noses when a terrier smelt him in a stack of straw. I have admired him as he breaks from the covert, races across the shining field and dives into the stream to put hounds off the scent. I have delighted as Charlie, seeing hounds hunting as they should with their noses and not their eyes, has doubled back and danced past the unseeing pack within a few feet of it.

'The fox is wild and very alive, and this is what you love and respect, though (because?) you want him dead. Perhaps we should reverse Oscar Wilde and say that each man loves the thing he kills.

'And when the fox is dead, it is sad. The death is virtually instantaneous, so the :tearing apart alive" that antis complain of, doesn't happen. But he is torn apart dead, "broken up", so that hounds may have blood and hunt well next time. It is melancholy to see his body afterwards, sometimes in two parts, stretched and muddy and grey – very, very dead, like the animals in Chardin's late still-lifes. Strange that word "still-life" when speaking of the dead.

'Anyhow, I shall be up and hunting again as soon as it thaws…'

MUDDY PETTICOATS

A most delightful nineteenth century hunting story concerns a young lady called Miss Augusta Tawke, who one day in November accompanied a friend to a meet of the Beaufort outside Bath.

Miss Tawke's friend was a pretty girl of about nineteen, married to a cavalry officer. She was a terrible rider and her husband made her swear she would not go hunting.

'My friend was tall and handsome, with a very elegant figure, and quantities of fair hair very loosely dressed,' Miss Tawke recalled in her hunting memoirs. 'She was quite unaccustomed to riding, and sitting rather as one may say on "tiptoe". The habit was very long and the skirt full, and looking below the waist it was quite evident that she had not removed her ordinary garments. She wore a lovely hat and long white feather'.

The pair arrived at the meet just as the field was setting off. They had no intention of joining in, but Miss Tawke's friend could not contain herself. She was seized with an impulse to follow.

'She called out to me: "Come on Augusta", and off she went, the groom and I following. We soon came to a small bank; on the far side of which was a very heavy ploughed field: over this obstacle she flew. I saw the figure toppling and toppling, and at last, quite unable to recover herself, off she came, was flung over her horse's head, and landed in the ploughed field some yards away. She was quite unhurt, but terribly crestfallen. I was choking with laughter...the lovely hat and long white feather had flown away; the beautiful hair hanging down her back. The skirt, which had got much out of place, displayed fine frilled petticoats ; her small feet in shoes – with sandals – and the white open-worked stockings plastered with mud'.

Miss Tawke concluded that when they rode back into Bath they held their heads low because of 'the sorry sight we presented as we rode through the most fashionable streets – just as the beau monde was taking a morning airing'.

From Hunting Recollections *by Miss Tawke, Francis and Sons, 1911*

SMART FOX

ARE FOXES BRIGHTER ACROSS THE ATLANTIC? An MFH in Virginia noted in 1926 how, during a four hour run, a fox 'deliberately led the pack over every bad scenting spot he could pick out; he walked on rocks for a half mile; he traversed over three miles of stone walls, and in one place walked a rail fence for three hundred yards, retracing his own steps to add to the fun'.

LUCK

EIGHTEENTH CENTURY hunting scribe Peter Beckford tells the story of a huntsman who was so drunk during a hunt one morning that he got off his horse in a wood and went to sleep on the ground while hounds disappeared from view. 'However, he had great good luck on his side,' Beckford explains, 'For at the very instant he was found, a fox was halloed'. The huntsman mounted his horse, found his hounds and killed his fox. The Master instantly forgave him.

HUNTING U.S.A.

AMERICA'S HUNTING CAPITAL is Middleburg, Virginia, a small town utterly devoted to the chase.

Middleburg, population 600, has built an entire industry around foxhunting in the same way that Melton Mowbray did over a century ago.

Everything in Middleburg is to do with hunting, from the fox and horn motif on the police department vehicles, to the town's main hostelry, The Red Fox Inn, billed as the oldest original inn in the United States. The town's top main visitor attraction is the National Sporting Library, a 17,000 book collection covering all field sports but mostly hunting; the annual Christmas parade features Santa followed by the horses and hounds of the Middleburg Hunt. And it is said that by the age of ten most of the children at the town's Foxcroft School are learning to ride to hounds.

Middleburg was established in 1787 a trading post on a main route through Virginia.

Hunting began in the area around 1840 with the founding of the Piedmont Foxhounds, but the craze did not take off properly until the early twentieth century when thousands began to descend on Virginia's rolling hills around Middleburg and Warrenton for hunting and steeplechasing.

There are five hunts operating in the country around Middleburg – the Piedmont, the Middleburg, the Orange County, The M.O.C. (Middleburg Orange County), and the Snickersville. Middleburg historian Vicky Moon says, 'A fanatic – and there are a few – could go out seven days a week... Foxhunting is the inner core of life in Middleburg. It's the original glue that held this community together.'

• Jackie Kennedy used to ride to hounds at Middleburg in the early 1960s. Jackie and JFK leased the Glen Ora estate south of Middleburg, only two hours drive from Washington, as a hideaway to escape the pressures of the White House. Glen Ora, in uppercrust Virginia horse country, suited Jackie perfectly. Her favoured hunt was the Orange County. The President and his wife eventually built their own house called Wexford, named after the town of Kennedy's Irish roots.

FAINT WOOF

BIG DRAMA towards the end of the 1950 season when two over-enthusiastic hounds from the Western Hunt ended up at the bottom of an abandoned mineshaft at Nacledra, Cornwall. Master Leslie Oats sounded his hunting horn at the head of the shaft. Eventually a faint answering bark was heard echoing from the darkness below. Mr Oats was lowered 100 feet down. He found the hounds huddling in a tunnel and they were hauled to the surface.

BLACK SHEEP, WELL-FED HOUNDS

The 'reckless extravagance' of a well-connected master of hounds kept the British public amused in the year leading up to the First World War. Mr. Allan Havelock-Allan, Master of the West Kent, ended up in the London bankruptcy court in 1913 owing nearly £5000, a hefty sum in those days.

The court heard that Havelock-Allan had blown a £90,000 inheritance on the Stock Exchange, racing and hunting. £5000 alone had been squandered on chemin de fer in Le Touquet. He admitted that he had been living hopelessly beyond his means and hoped to recoup his losses by eventually winning at cards. This had failed to happen. His only income now was a £200 a year allowance from his disapproving older brother, Sir Henry Havelock-Allan, Bt., a Liberal politician, who was Under-Secretary of State for India.

None of the above had stopped Havelock-Allan from pursuing his great love: hunting. Even on his uppers he had borrowed £1000 from members of the West Kent committee in order to keep the foxhounds going. It was noted in court that his excessive expenditure 'was partly due to his having given the hounds the very best food'.

> • The wretched Allan Havelock-Allan lived in the shadow of not only his brother but also his father Sir Henry Havelock-Allan, 1st Baronet, who as a twenty-six-year-old lieutenant in India won the Victoria Cross for capturing an enemy gun during the 1857 Indian Mutiny at Cawnpore.

DANGEROUS GROUND

The author is amused by an old joke told in Quorn country about a man who bragged about how well he knew the Melton hunting set and was asked if he knew Barkby Holt. 'Yes, of course, I dined with him last week.' Barkby Holt is one of the Quorn's most celebrated coverts, and the name of a famous Quorn run of 1903.

OLD BAG

MELTON MOWBRAY socialite the Countess of Wilton (1836-1919) suffered so badly from eczema during cold weather that out hunting she wore two veils, one white and one black, with a silk bag over her nose. Known as the Queen of Melton, Lady Wilton was still riding with the Quorn at the age of eighty.

SHIFTER AND TIPLER

THE EARLIEST HOUND BREEDING BOOKS were kept by Mr Orlebar of Hinwick Hall, Bedfordshire, in the 1700s. Orlebar was famous for two exceptional hounds, Shifter and Tipler. The first record of a pack of hounds being sold was in 1730, when a Dorset squire Thomas Fowne sold his pack to a Yorkshireman called Mr. Bowles. By 1750 there were around fifty hound breeders in England, led by the 5th Duke of Beaufort.

OUTWITTING FOXES

EARTH-STOPPING was one of the more controversial hunting activities of pre-ban days. Earths would be blocked so that foxes could not go to ground while they were being chased. With the 1992 Protection of Badgers Act earth-stopping came in for more flak because of the tendency of foxes to seek refuge in badger earths. The law decreed that you must never interfere with a badger earth.

Ronnie Wallace (1919–2002), one of the twentieth century's greatest foxhunters and known for his extraordinary skills in casting hounds, spent a remarkable fifty-eight consecutive seasons of Mastership at the Heythrop and the Exmoor. Here he explains why earth-stopping is so important to hunting:

'Earth-stopping is not a dirty trick dreamed up by foxhunters to outwit foxes. It produces what is best in hunting. Since hounds must kill foxes, how much better that this be done in a clean, fair hunt than by a local mining party. If all foxes were merely chased into holes and then dug out, who among us would call it good sport? Without earthstopping, that is the alternative.

'It is no use saying that one could just take off one's hat to that fox, say Goodnight and go home, because realities must be faced. Somebody will be tempted to return to the earth and snare or gas him next day. Foxes have a better chance of escape above the ground than below it...

'Earthstopping, efficiently conducted, results in foxes exploring more country, and therefore in better sport....if foxes know that earths are habitually stopped, they will not waste time in circling to test out the earthstopper, but get away quickly.

'Now that the Badger Act is in force, Hunts have no choice but to stop earths if they are to have success. If they do not, the foxes simply pour down badger setts...and the badgers are disturbed from their winter slumbers.

'Stopping badger setts does not disturb the badgers...the badger population has increased considerably despite centuries of earthstopping. Many people seem not to realise that badgers have several holiday homes. They will leave their main earth when perhaps it has become too much lived-in, and are then to be found in a brand new place probably not far away. Although foxes like to live with badgers, the reverse is not so. Badgers would rather not have foxes on the premises. Sow badgers will drive foxes away when they have cubs, and sometimes kill them. If fox cubs are found with their skulls crushed or ribs broken, a badger will invariably be the culprit.'

From A Manual Of Foxhunting, *by Ronnie Wallace, Swan Hill Press, 2003*

• Unlike many other masters, who employed professional huntsmen, Ronnie Wallace hunted hounds himself well into his seventies. He was regarded as a legend by his peers. A fellow MFH remarked, 'We call him God, don't we?' God or not, he had a quick temper and was prone to refer to an erring member of the field as 'a poached egg'. People would hide behind a hedge rather than be discovered in the wrong place at the wrong time. Wallace was not a great rider and, like all truly great MFHs, considered horses little more than a means of conveyance for hunting hounds. Having hunted his first fox at eleven, he realised he had found his reason for living. But he recalled later he had 'hated the pony'. Wallace was on his way to see his wife Rosie in hospital at Taunton, Somerset, in February, 2002, when he was killed in a car crash. He was eighty-two.

• Ronnie Wallace achieved a record season in his last year as Master of the Eton College Beagles in 1936. The pack hunted 104 days, accounting for 75 brace of hares and three foxes, figures which have never been surpassed. On the opening meet hounds went off piste and killed a fox in a kitchen. Wallace's picture appeared in newspapers and was seen by a woman, an 'anti' from Bracknell. 'You have a very sweet face,' she wrote to him. 'Can I not save you before it's too late?'

TO FOXHUNTING

By 1890, Lord Spencer, Master of the Pytchley, was so fed up with the huge fields – up to 500 riders, with numerous followers – that he tried to ban Brooksby, *The Field's* famous hunting correspondent. The problem was the vast numbers of social climbers flocking to Leicestershire. People were turning up simply to get their names in the magazine. Brooksby irritated Spencer by refusing to stop attending the meets, but he did agree to refrain from naming individual riders.

'Brooksby' was the pen-name of ex-cavalry officer Captain Edward Pennell Elmhirst, who took his monicker from a cousin's house in Leicestershire. He took his hunting seriously, both the chase and the social side.

Armed with a bottle of champagne and a cigar, he would write up the day that evening while events were fresh in memory. He admitted he could not recall the nuances of the day 'until my nose is wreathed in smoke'. And never in his life did he open a bottle of fizz without drinking a toast to foxhunting.

A series of falls left Brooksby crippled by his late sixties. He died in 1916 at the age of seventy-one. A friend remarked, 'When he could go not go out hunting, life for him held nothing more'.

• Brooksby held views that did not always endear him to his readers. He described the digging out of foxes when they went to ground as 'a disgrace to a noble sport'.

A HIGH NOTED BITCH ON A

This description of how hounds 'sing' in kennel appeared in *A Huntsman's Log Book* by the Anglo-American hound breeder Isaac 'Ikey' Bell, acknowledged as the creator of the modern foxhound. Bell claimed that hounds usually tune to the key of A:

'It is always started by a single hound, and gradually more and more hounds "tune in", and in the same way it gradually subsides as odd ones drop out, until silence reigns in the night once more. Later on…another individual, not necessarily the hound who started the tune on the last occasion, and probably one with a different pitch of note, will set them all off again.

'…The singing is always in harmony like it is in an orchestra, and tuned to the note of the hound which began it. For instance, should the music be started by a high-noted bitch on A (which is the more usual note), the deepest-voiced doghounds will take it up on A on a lower octave, while others will take it in "thirds" and "sixths", and so it continues to swell and grow in perfect orchestral harmony and there is never a discordant note heard.

'I was not surprised to learn this, for know from experience that a hound's ear is most senstive, and that a "discord" blown on the horn causes hounds mental pain. Such a discord on the horn is used by huntsmen to admonish a hound when rioting, and it invariably stops him. I used to use this method at one time, but gave it up, as I found it was apt to distress the others, and unless the whole pack were seriously misbehaving, I would not recommend it.'

DEATH IN THE MIDST OF LIFE

THE GREATEST LOSS OF HUMAN LIFE on a hunting field happened on 4 February 1869.

In what became known as the Newby Ferry Disaster four members of the York and Ainsty and two boatmen drowned after an overloaded river ferry capsized midstream.

The day had started well with a meet in glorious sunshine at South Stainley, followed by an hour's run to the banks of the River Ure. Participants said later it was one of the best morning's hunting they'd had in a long time. Given the choice of being caught by the hounds or swimming the river, the fox sensibly chose the latter course and dived into the water. The pack followed. Powter, the second whip swung round by Boroughbridge to stop the hounds, but the Master, Sir Charles Slingsby, and twelve other horsemen made a fatal error and piled onto the small chain ferry across the river. The craft was intended for only four horses and turned turtle midstream.

The tragedy was written up later in *The Field* by hunt member Thomas Clayton who witnessed the hounds being washed over the weir above the ferry crossing point 'like so many herrings…But they soon recovered, and, true to their kind, picked up the scent on the opposite bank, and were in full cry during the time of the catastrophe'. Miraculously, only one hound was drowned.

Clayton reported that it was Sir Charles, carried away by the thrill of the chase, who ordered his fellow horsemen onto the ferry. 'The horses were closely packed, like bullocks in a bullock-truck. The boat swayed once or twice, and then turned completely over for several seconds leaving nothing to the view but the bottom of the boat. It seemed impossible that any could be saved, but by degrees heads began to appear'.

Immediately the boat began to lean, Sir Charles's horse Saltfish jumped over the side. But one of his hind legs became entangled with the chains. 'The next thing I saw was Sir Charles about the horse's head, both struggling for life,' Clayton continued. 'In a few seconds I saw him buffeting in the boiling gulf. He turned on his back, and seemed to be making for some overhanging trees on the north shore. I called to him to "cheer up".'

Clayton's jolly hockey sticks encouragement came to naught. Sir Charles swam about ten yards from the bank when the icy current swept him away and he was drowned. Saltfish followed him for a few moments, but then seemed to think better of it. He turned and struggled to the shore where he managed to pull himself out of the water.

Back at the ferry there was chaos. 'A life and death fight with men and horses underneath.' Six people had drowned: Sir Charles, Edward Lloyd, Edward Robinson, the first whip William Orvis, and the two boatmen, Christopher Warriner and his son James.

Robinson had a particularly nasty end. A non-swimmer, he clung to his horse, which dragged him down. 'His screams were terrible,' reported Clayton. 'He emitted two fearful shrieks and then went under.'

The heroes of the day were three surviving horsemen: Robert Vyner, Richard Thompson and a Mr Ingilby from Ripley. Having managed to hang onto the ferry, Vyner and Ingilby jumped into the river and tried in vain to save Lloyd. Thompson jumped in, and tried to save Slingsby. But the water was so cold he was forced to give up.

Luckiest man of the day was a Major Mussenden, of the 8th Hussars. Clayton wrote, 'He had the most extraordinary escapes ever man had. Twice he sank right among the horses, and twice rose. His head was kicked, and his coat nearly torn off his back, but he was pulled into the boat.' Saddest sight of the day was that of the second whipper-in, all alone in the fields, returning hounds to kennels.

With the flourish of a true Victorian, Clayton added grimly, 'The beginning of the tragedy to the end was not more than two or three minutes – a vivid illustration of sacred writ, that in the midst of life we are in death.'

The day after the accident hunting throughout England was suspended as a mark of respect. The York and Ainsty hunted no more that season, but the Bramham Moor and the Holderness each had a day in the country by invitation. Enormous crowds turned out to pay their respects.

• A month after the Newby Ferry Disaster, it was reported coldly in the York and Ainsty annals that the horses of the three dead foxhunters achieved exceptionally good prices at auction. Sir Charles's mounts were sold during a 'blinding snowstorm' at his family seat Scriven Park, near Knaresborough. His own horses did well though 'some of the servants' horses were stale and a little worn...and the brood mares made bad prices, and were not a very fashionable lot'.

• The Victorian poets had a high, gloomy old time with the Newby Ferry Disaster. Cheshire landowner and hunting bard Rowland Edgerton-Warburton produced the following excruciating lines:

> 'Let Yorkshire, while England re-echoes her wail
> Bereft of her bravest, record the sad tale;
> How Slingsby, of Scriven, at Newby fell
> In the heat of the chase that he loved so well.'

BEEF ON THE RIB

THE SECOND HORSE SYSTEM is said to have been perfected by Lord Sefton during his Mastership of the Quorn, 1800–1805.

Known as Lord Dashalong for his fondness for fast carriages, William Molyneux, 2nd Earl of Sefton was a gambling pal of the Prince Regent. He was a huge man. A Quorn historian wrote, 'His weight, which eventually caused him to give up fox-hunting altogether, enabled him to bore his way through the thickest blackthorn fences in his country. But he was a capital hand at getting over a country.'

Sefton's bulk made his horses tire easily, so he ensured that he had at least three mounts ready in his wake. Other stag and foxhunters had used second horses in the past (Henry VIII is said to have used eight) but they were usually stationed at the back of the field. Sefton insisted that his grooms remained close by him so that he could swap at a moment's notice. 'He changed from one to the other… about every fifteen or twenty minutes, though on one occasion one of his best horses, Loadstar, carried his owner for an hour and five minutes.'

Sefton gave up hunting when his vast size meant he could no longer find horses to carry him as fast as he wished to go. He instead pursued his other loves: racing and coursing. His gambling obsession took its toll – a critic described him as a 'gigantic hunchback who lost largely on all occasions' – and he was forced to sell of part of his estates, including land at Aintree to found a steeplechase course.

• The sporting satirist Edward Goulburn had great fun with Sefton with this 1807 ditty:

> 'Earl Sefton came next, and for beef on the rib
> No Leicestershire bullock was rounder ;
> A wonderful weight at a wonderful rate,
> He flew like a twenty-four pounder.'

• Sefton was by no means the largest man in Quorn country. Fanatical hunting man Daniel Lambert, master of Leicester Gaol, weighed no less than fifty-two stone, though the Quorn historian pointed out, 'Owing to his weight, he could not participate in any branch of the chase other than otter-hunting'.

• By the 1830s the second horse system had been greatly improved, according to the hunting journalist Nimrod. 'The second horseman now rides to points instead of following the hounds, and thus often meets his master at a most favourable moment, when his good steed is sinking, with one that has not been out of a trot. There is much humanity as well as comfort in this arrangement, for at the pace hounds now go over the grass countries, horses become distressed under heavy weights, in a short time after the chase begins, when the scent lies well, and they are manfully ridden up to the pack.'

• 'There is no class of person who gets a Hunt into disrepute more than second horsemen. These, as a rule, are stable helpers dressed up in livery, extremely thoughtless, and noted for leaving gates open and very often jumping their masters' horses over fences. The strictest orders possible should be given to them, not once, but several times during the season.'

Edwardian hunting writer C. F. P. McNeill, The Unwritten Laws of Foxhunting, *1905*

PUPPY CULT

A LANDOWNER called Charles Pelham, later the first Lord Yarborough, started the cult of puppy walking on his Lincolnshire estate Brocklesby. His tenants were strongly encouraged (ordered?) to take in hound puppies and bring them on until they were old enough to join the pack. Whether all the Brocklesby tenants were thrilled to introduce unruly hound pups into their lives is unknown, but a history of the Brocklesby Hounds notes that 'there are no better puppy-walkers, no keener fox-preservers, and no finer sportsmen than the tenant farmers in North Lincolnshire'.

Not all puppy-walking went according to plan at Brocklesby. In 1836 a gamekeeper shot dead a puppy being walked by a farmer called Mr. Empson. The Brocklesby historian complains, 'Even in those days "velveteens" were apt to be troublesome'. (Shooting men were nicknamed velveteens because of their velvet coats.)

FOX DROP

The greatest drop achieved by a fox without hurting itself happened on 19 February 1886 in Blackmore Vale country. The fox had escaped the pack by climbing to the top of an elm tree. There he stuck until dislodged by the second whipper-in, an expert tree-climber. Charlie dropped forty-four feet onto his nose. Miraculously, he got up and ran two miles before being killed by hounds.

COLONIAL RELIC

SADDAM HUSSEIN banned hunting in Iraq because people who hunted were 'bloodsuckers'. He conveniently ignored the fact that his sons and many of his henchmen were keen shots.

During the monarchy in pre-Saddam days, there was a regular fox and wild boar hunt in the palm groves near the river Tigris with a pack of Salukis and Afghan hounds. The staff of the British Embassy in Baghdad would arrive at meets dressed in hunting red as for Leicestershire. The season lasted during the cool period between March and April.

After Saddam came to power landowners no longer had the money to hunt. English-style hunting was a disliked relic of Iraq's colonial past. Eventually the Revolutionary Command Council banned the sport on spurious environmental grounds.

BOW-WOWING AT THE SKY

THIS SPLENDIDLY CATTY DESCRIPTION of a pack of French foxhounds appeared in an 1835 London publication called *The Mirror of Literature, Amusement and Instruction*. The writer, Reuben Percy, had just returned from a foxhunting jaunt in the South of France…

'I have seen one or two dogs good enough to have held a respectable place, even in an English pack; but the generality are good for nothing. They never hunt with what we should call courage, but potter about like a parcel of pigs in an Indian corn-field. Often have I been amused by observing some of them, when unable to pick up the scent, sit down on their hind-quarters, and, with their noses in the air, composedly "bow-wow" away at the skies. But one cannot, considering their training, blame them for this. In one particular, I think, they are superior to our dogs, and that is, that their notes are even more musical than those of our dogs; but this, I believe, is owing to the climate – for I have been informed that English dogs, after having been some time in France, acquire the same melody of sound. They are totally dissimilar in appearance: there is the heavy, strong, muscular animal, more adapted for a bear-hunt; the long-backed, greyhound looking brute; and a cur, something like the beagle in sweet confusion blended.'

BLOCK AND MALLET

U NTIL THE FIRST WORLD WAR the ears of many hounds were
rounded, or trimmed, in the same way a tail might be docked.
Rounded ears were meant to protect them from being torn by sharp
undergrowth and hedges.

In 1920, hunting supremo Lord Willoughby de Broke wrote that rounding
'is a relic of an age when mutilation of animals for the sake of appearance was
much more common than it is to-day'.

There were two sides to the argument. The rounders said that doctored
ears stopped them from being ripped by thorns. The anti-rounders claimed
that nature gave hounds long ears to protect the ear-hole from getting water
in it. Whatever the case, rounding was a messy business with much blood
spilled in the process. Victorian harrier expert Henry Ryden said that rounding
should be done when puppies were six months old. 'The ceremony should
take place before the weather…rounding may be done with scissors, or with
a special instrument (shaped like a crescent and a block and mallet'.

Willoughby de Broke hated the practice. 'The silken ear of the Hound,
untouched by the knife, lying close to his head, tapering down to a delicate
point, is surely one of nature's endowments which cannot be improved by
human interference.'

• There is doubt over when the practice of rounding began in English kennels.
The few hound pictures of animal painter Francis Barlow (1626–1702) show
no rounded ears, but the many pictures of John Wooton (1685–1765) do.
Stephen Elmer's 1780 portrait of the England's greatest ever hound Trojan of
the Warwickshire shows him with closely rounded ears.

WISDOM

'Wisdom is a fox who after long hunting will at last cost
you the pains to dig out'.

Jonathan Swift

LADY CYCLISTS

THE EMERGENCE OF THE BICYCLE towards the end of the nineteenth century caused problems at meets . Hunts complained that cyclists were obstructing horses and hounds.

Hunting journalist George Underhill, author of a book of 'practical hints to hunting men' wrote in 1900: 'It has been a constant complaint that the fashionable meets of hounds are attended by crowds of foot-people and cyclists, whose only motives are idle curiosity and the eclat of saying afterwards that they have been out with hounds. I commend their ambition to see hounds, though I wish that they would learn the rudiments of "the noble science".'

Underhill noted that only a few years earlier foot followers had been country people who knew the correct form. 'Now they are the outpourings of excursion trains,' he sniffed.

The worst offenders were female cyclists.

'The pity is that these ladies wish to assert their independence of fox-hunting etiquette by attempting to follow hounds on their machines. A meet may be considered as a public spectacle, like a review of troops, but when hounds move off to draw their first covert the spectacle should be at an end so far as the cycling contingent is concerned. Yet I have seen ladies trying to thread their way down a narrow lane through a cavalcade of excited horses at the risk of being kicked to death.'

HUNTING DRILL BOOK

Perhaps the most significant huntsman of them all was Thomas Smith, Master of the Craven Hounds in Berkshire in the 1830s, before moving to the Pytchley. He was famous for the Tom Smith Cast, a patent way of casting hounds, and was the first person to produce a diagram showing the casting of hounds.

The Victorian hunting fraternity regarded casting as a science. Smith developed the 'all round my hat' cast, based on the principle of first sending hounds the way you don't think the fox has gone. Smith killed ninety foxes in ninety-one days while with the Craven, a remarkable achievement in a hunt which had no reputation as a scenting country. A fellow master remarked, 'I would sooner have a pack of hounds behind me than Tom Smith with a stick in his hand'.

It has been said that if a huntsman should read only one book in his life it should be Smith's *Diary Of A Huntsman*. Whereas the hunting author Peter Beckford gave his readers witty paragraphs, Smith told you how to hunt properly.

Diary Of A Huntsman included an 'autobiography' of Wily, a fox who has a running conversation with his landowner: 'Our walks in life are different; 'tis yours to ride, 'tis mine to run; 'tis yours to pursue, 'tis mine to be pursued; we shall meet again in the field, the horn will sound the alarm, my appearance will be greeted with a view halloo that shall set the blood of hundreds in motion! Whether after that day of trial I shall again sit among my listening cubs and relate to them how many peers, parsons and squires lay prostrate on the turf and were soused in the brook while pursuing my glorious course, or whether my brush shall at length adorn your Lordship's hat, fate must decide…'

SIN

'Fox-terriers are born with about four times as much original sin in them as other dogs.'

*English writer and humourist Jerome K. Jerome
(1859–1927)*

DREAMS

'A sleeping fox counts hens in his dreams.'

Russian proverb

HOW TO AVOID MAKING ENEMIES

Strict words from the Master of Foxhounds Association
on how hunt followers should behave...

❧ Make every effort to avoid causing damage to land, fences or crops. Damage must be reported to an appropriate hunt official;

❧ Close all gates and avoid disturbance to livestock. Sometimes gates appear to be permanently open, but if in doubt close them; Do not ride or drive on mown verges, or ride several abreast through villages and along busy roads;

❧ Do not cause obstruction when parking vehicles, horseboxes or trailers at any time;

❧ Do not park on both sides of roads and so interrupt the flow of other traffic. Help and acknowledgement must be afforded to passing traffic. Remember every delayed motorist or lorry driver becomes a potential enemy of hunting;

❧ Do not park or drive on private land without the express permission of the landholder.

ANTIQUATED IDEAS

1899 saw the publication of spoof titled *Foxhunting: A Treatise*, by an author calling himself The Rt. Hon. The Earl of Kilreynard. Though some thicker members of the hunting set took the book seriously, it didn't take much to deduce that the name Kilreynard was a joke. The book was actually written by an amateur humorist called C. W. Bell, who donated the proceeds to the Hunt Servants' Benefit Society.

Here are some of Kilreynard's observations:

- 'There can be no question that the glacial periods of the dark ages proved most disastrous to the interests of foxhunting when we consider the discouragement that five thousand or more years of unbroken frost would cause even the most enthusiastic devotee.'

- 'Earnest discussions as to how hounds should be "handled", coverts drawn, and casts made are of frequent occurrence in the hunting field, making the duties of the professional huntsman a matter of ease. Antiquated ideas as to the movements of a flock of sheep, the carrion crow, or jay being an indication as to a fox's movements have long since vanished.'

- 'The Master of Foxhounds… should know something of the habits of the fox beyond what he has learnt from the early perusal of *Aesop's Fables*. He should know where a fox will go to when pursued by hounds. Failing this, the next best thing is the ability to maintain that he knows, whether he does or not.'

- 'A knowledge of horseflesh is most useful to a Master of Hounds, although he should always refrain from obtruding it on his stud groom, to whom the buying and selling of hunters should be left entirely. The Master should be able to preserve as good a balance at his bankers as he does on horseback.'

- 'The drop fence. When this kind of obstacle presents itself there is a good opportunity to perpetrate a harmless joke. Urge some short-sighted friend to "go on," assuring him that it is nothing. Afterwards, when you have picked him up, you remark, in a jocular manner, that he appears to have had a "drop too much". This is a fine witticism, and cannot fail to provoke great merriment amongst all present.'

❧ 'Seeds may be ridden over by the novice, and no previous knowledge of foxhunting is required, besides which the feat is quite free from all danger, if practised during the absence of the agriculturist to whom the field belongs. The same may be safely said of the ewe pen.'

❧ 'A wheat field invariably has great attractions for hard-riding men in wet weather, particularly if a gap in the fence makes it easy of access.'

❧ 'Jumping on hounds has more to do with the "field" than the master. It is a time-honoured custom, and, although unpopular with huntsmen, it holds its own as an amusement to be indulged in after a hunt breakfast.'

❧ 'To harbour a feeling of compassion for a fallen hero, be he never so handsome, is a weakness that should be scorned by modern sportswomen. To dismount and raise the unconscious head upon her lap, bathing the pale forehead with eau de Cologne, is only worthy of the heroine of a sporting novel. When the fractured collar-bone is mended, he will be off, like a butterfly back to the field, leaving behind him only a broken heart.'

❧ 'Do not enquire at the Quorn kennels whether they still hunt both hare and fox.'

GALLOPING SNORES

A young country Squire requested my hand
Whose joy 'twas to ride by my side,
So domestic a prospect what girl could withstand?
I became truly willing his bride.

The Honeymoon scarcely her soft beams withdrew,
When my loved tete-a-tete I must yield,
For Autumn arrived, and my rivals I knew
In the birds and the beasts of the field.

Each day I must roam alone in the grounds
And converse with my husband no more,
For away he went galloping after the hounds
And returned in the evening to snore.

The Fox-Hunting Husband, from Lyra Venatica,
a collection of hunting songs compiled by
John Sherard Reeve, 1906

RIGHT PEOPLE

'It isn't mere convention. Everyone can see that the people
who hunt are the right people and the people who don't are
the wrong ones.'

George Bernard Shaw, Heartbreak House *(1920)*

CIRCUS DOGS

RUNNING HOUNDS were considered such great entertainment in eighteenth century England that in 1793 a pack was introduced to a London circus. The Royal Circus, in Blackfriars, on the south bank, was run by a man called Hughes who employed fifteen couples to chase a stag round the auditorium by lamp-light. The spectacle was meant to be a representation of the King's stag hunt at Windsor, complete with the ceremony of turning out the deer and the chase to the death. The hunt staff in the show were dressed in Royal uniform. Much to the theatregoers' delight the exhausted quarry would eventually succumb to the hounds, whereupon the antlers were sawn off.

A critic from *The Times* wrote, 'This novelty brought a considerable concourse to the Circus last night, and the performance received the most universal marks of approbation. It is, in truth, a most charming spectacle.'

Despite the cheers, many people considered the show pretty unsporting. It also cost a fortune to put on and didn't last long. A few years later Hughes was bankrupt.

UNSUITABLE AMUSEMENT

AT THE OUTBREAK OF THE FIRST WORLD WAR 170,000 horses were moblised, most of them from the hunting field.

War was declared on 4 August 1914 just as cub hunting started. The War Office requested horses for the cavalry. Within ten days 15,000 hunters were ready for departure. Lawn meets were cancelled and scarlet coats were moth balled.

Hunting narrowly escaped being banned. It was saved only after the farming lobby complained that foxes would run rampant. Also, more flippantly, senior Army staff noted that officers would not be able to relax on leave from the front if there was no hunting. Hunting was a 'first class national asset'.

It was not until 1917 that serious restrictions were placed on the sport. On 8 February Captain Charles Bathurst for the Government's Food Controller's Department announced that Masters of foxhounds had agreed to reduce substantially the number of days' hunting throughout England and Wales. They were prepared too to slaughter a large proportion of hounds. Some Masters even advised their members to shoot foxes in order to prevent the destruction of poultry.

At the front, some enterprising cavalry regiments imported packs of hounds into France during the winter of 1914. The South Irish Horse kept a tame fox which they fed on chicken. It was released in the front of hounds which were called off the moment they looked like killing it. The SIH's fun ended when another nameless regiment claimed the creature, saying that they had brought it over from England as a mascot.

The top brass thought it best to ban hunting behind the trenches after the French complained that the British weren't taking the war seriously. French farmers objected to British cavalry officers ruining their crops. A stuffy French directive stated: 'It is not suitable to have such amusement in a devastated country or when that country is a foreign land to those that hunt'. The latter part of this statement implied that it might have been acceptable had it been French officers hunting.

Some regiments gave two fingers to *les Frogs* and carried on regardless. There were rumours that the 1st Battalion Royal Fusiliers were pursuing hares and foxes with hounds in 'the Somme back area' as late as 1917.

Further away, in Salonika, the Scottish Horse formed a scratch pack which met every Saturday to hunt hares behind the trenches 'war permitting'. Other field sports flourished during the hostilities. In 1917 the Mesopotamia Comforts Fund for British Troops made an appeal for fishing rods. And back in France some cavalry officers discovered that it was good fun riding down partridges with polo mallets.

• When Captain Oskar Teichman, DSO, MC, of the Royal Army Medical Corps, returned to Belah, Palestine, in early 1918 he found hunting was 'in full swing'. The Belah Hounds (Fifth Mounted Brigade) were meeting three days a week south of the Wadi, while the Gaza Hounds (Twenty-second Mounted Brigade) hunted the country to the north. 'The hounds consisted chiefly of terriers and native dogs', Teichman recalled in his memoirs. 'But the Sherwood Rangers actually possessed one couple of foxhounds. As a rule the jackal had to be finally dispatched by one of the whips before hounds would break him up, which made the end of the hunt somewhat tame. On one occasion a jackal was hunted from a fig grove outside our camp to Ali Muntar, where he went aground in an old tomb, the distance traversed being about seven or eight miles.' On 16 March 1918, the Seventh Brigade held a 'most successful' point to point in the countryside outside Gaza. Invitations were issued to all units in the vicinity. 'Our C.O. drove our H.Q. Mess over in a light ambulance wagon drawn by four horses, our trumpeter-major tootling the horn', Teichman wrote. 'Even at this stage of the war a certain number of horses well known in the locality turned out to compete. The course was a good one, and regulation fences had been erected. The race of the day, the Palestine Grand National, which had last year been run just before the Battle of Rafa, was again secured by a horse owned by a Warwickshire squadron leader.'

From The Diary of a Yeomanry M.O. *by Captain O. Teichmann,*
T Fisher Unwin 1921

• Before 1914 there were 426 packs hunting in Britain. By 1939 there were 401. Not bad considering the devastation of the war and the taxation that followed.

• There were no less than thirty-seven Masters of Foxhounds, mostly from the West Country, on the troopship *Olympic* taking 4000 men from Britain to the Dardanelles for the 1915 Gallipoli campaign. On their way out, the MFHs had an informal dinner. At the end of the meal a hunting horn was handed round and everybody asked to blow into it...with embarrassing results. Out of thirty-seven foxhunters, only three could blow a horn. Their excuse was that nearly all employed professional huntsmen and therefore had no reason to blow a horn themselves. The first MFH to be killed at Gallipoli was Major Morland Gregg of the Devon and Somerset whose head was blown off by a shell that failed to explode.

NEAR TO PERFECTION

'THE NINETEENTH CENTURY was the first golden era of foxhunting and the hounds of that period were probably as near to perfection as possible for the job they were called upon to do. There was no wire; cattle were wintered in yards and sheep mostly folded so the fields were "clean"; there were no artifical manures; roads were gravelled and there were no cars or tractors to pump petrol or diesel fumes into hounds noses, and to "head" the fox on every possible occasion.'

Lt. Col. Sir Peter Farquhar (1904–1986), Master of the Portman in Dorset and one of the twentieth century's most distinguished hound breeders

PROPER SCREAMING

'I've only ever had one proper screaming argument with an animal rights activist. That was a great night. It was at a student party. She told me she believed animal lives to be worth just as much as human lives. I told her she was the most apathetically selfish person I'd ever met.'

Hugo Rifkind, on the failure of the Hunting Act, The Times, *2009*

MONARCH FOR THE DAY

'HE MAY BE RIGHT AND HE MAY BE WRONG, but all must acknowledge that the word of the Master is absolute law. If such are his opinions he has a perfect right to them… he is, in fact, recognised by all the sporting community as absolute monarch of the district for the day, and no one calling himself a sportsman or a gentleman would dispute the fact.'

Sir Hercules Langrishe, Bt., Master of the Kilkenny Fox Hounds at the turn of the nineteenth century. Sir Hercules was a fine player of the hunting horn, indeed of any metal tube that happened to be handy. His party trick was to play 'Gone away' on a gun barrel. A fine yachtsman as well as huntsman, he would study the wind in his casts. He believed that a fox 'tacked' to leeward, and he would hunt using this premise.

THE WISE OLD HOUND

Happy the man, who, with unrivall'd speed.

Can pass his fellows, and with pleasure view

The straggling pack; how, in the rapid course,

Alternate they preside, and, jostling, push

To guide the dubious scent; how giddy youth

Oft, babbling, errs, by wiser age reproved;

How, niggard of his strength, the wise old hound

Hangs in the rear, till some important point

Rouse all his diligence, or till the chase

Sinking he finds ; then to the head he springs.

With thirst of glory fired, and wins the prize.

From The Chase, *by William Somervile, 1804. Somervile (1675–1742) was a country gent turned poet with a family property in Worcestershire. (The Chase, a long poem that traced the history of hunting, was reprinted many times)*

ABSURDLY SMALL HEAD

'IT IS ALMOST WITH AWE that one reflects on the greatness of soul, the self-respect, the self-consciousness...of a very small terrier. Especially are these present in the terrier that is accredited to a pack of foxhounds. When it is considered what it can accomplish with that tiny rough body, those indomitable little legs, that absurdly small head, packed with constructive intelligence yet with a brain-pan no bigger than an apple, it is impossible to deny that its high opinion of itself is justified.'

From The Sweet Cry of Hounds *by Edith Somerville and Martin Ross (1936)*

Somerville and Ross were acclaimed Anglo-Irish writers famous for their Irish R. M. Series, about an ex-British Army officer who takes the post of Resident Magistrate in the west of Ireland at the end of the nineteenth century. The writers were cousins, both female. Martin Ross was a pseudonym for Edith Somerville's cousin Violet Martin. They embarked on the first Irish

R.M. book while Violet was confined to a sofa, recovering from a hunting fall. Violet died aged fifty-three of a brain tumour in 1915 but Somerville continued writing into old age using the Somerville and Ross byline. She communicated with her late partner through séances and believed Violet was helping her to write from beyond the grave. Edith's house at Castle Townshend, County Cork, was called Tally-Ho. She died aged ninety-two in 1949.

• Edith Somerville had the distinction of becoming Ireland's first lady master of foxhounds, with the West Carbery, 1903–08 and 1912–19. She spent much of her royalties on the pack.

• In the 1980s, the Irish R.M. books were turned into a Channel 4 television series starring the actor Peter Bowles. In one scene, the R.M's English wife is dancing with a stable-hand at a servants' ball. The stable hand suggests that 'The English and the Irish understand each other like the fox and the hound'.

The lady replies, 'But which is to which?'

'Ah, well,' says the stable hand. 'If we knew that, we'd know everything...'

DOG TEACHER

The title Master of Hounds was first used in the fourteenth century during the reign of Henry IV. The king's *Magister Canum* was paid a salary of 12 pence per day.

A MOST INDIFFERENT MEAL

Note that the following piece was written by an American Master of Foxhounds, proving that hunting attitudes are the same both sides of the Atlantic...

'The farmer's dinner...harks back to Victorian England when, as one writer put it: "The condescension of the hunting squirearchy in offering them food, drink and conversation was so flattering to farmers that they felt fully recompensed for past injuries'. Before the Second World War, Newbold Ely, MFH, editor of the national comic monthly *Judge* said that 'a Farmers' Dinner is a buffet affair at which a most indifferent meal is supposed to make the embarrassed and uncomfortable guests feel entirely all right about such items as broken fences, misplaced stock, trampled wheat and murdered poultry." Today we need a different approach. If the hunt want to organise such a party don't call it a Farmers' Dinner – this puts the people who give it in a different class from those invited. Some hunts use the term Landowners' Dinner. An even better title is to call it simply 'The Blankshire Hunt Barbecue' to which you invite virtually everyone on the fixture card list. Any attempt at being more selective can easily lead to trouble.'

From Foxhunting in North America,
by Alexander Mackay-Smith, MFH,
published by The American
Foxhound Club, 1985

BIDDABLE BABBLERS

Some hunting terms…

BABBLER: A noisy hound.

BIDDABLE: Hounds are biddable when they are totally responsive to their huntsman.

BILLETT: Fox excrement.

BOWLED OVER: When hounds have caught their fox above ground.

BREAK UP: When hounds kill the fox and eat its carcase.

BURST: The first, and, generally fastest part of the run, when fox, hound, horse, and man are at their freshest.

CARRY: To carry a good head is said of a pack of hounds crowding to a hot scent.

CAST : When the huntsman directs hounds to fan out in search of the scent of the quarry.

CHALLENGE: The hound which first speaks to the scent in covert is said to challenge.

CHECK: A stop in the run owing to a temporary loss of scent.

CHOP: A fox killed before he has had time to break cover is said to have been chopped.

COCKTAIL: Any horse not thoroughbred.

CROPPER: A bad fall. Can also use crumple and crowner. A truly bad fall on the head is an Imperial Crowner.

DRAG: The scent left by the fox returning home from his nightly prowling.

DRAW: The act of encouraging hounds through a covert in search of quarry.

FEATHER: The quivering stern (tail) of a hound when he scents his quarry but it not certain enough to give tongue.

FOIL: An animal runs its foils when it returns on its own tracks. Scent is foiled if it is spoilt for some reason, for instance if the quarry cross the line of other animals, a stream, or strong smelling fertiliser.

FORM: The seat, or kennel, of the hare.

GIVEN BEST: A fox is given best when hounds can no longer sustain the line, or when the huntsman decides to abandon the hunt. e.g. in failing light.

HARK-FORRARD: The huntsman's cheer to his hounds to encourage them on the scent.

HEEL LINE: Hounds are running a heel line when they are hunting the scent the reverse way, away from the fox, because they have hit the line at the wrong angle.

HOLDING UP: Positioning the field around the covert to keep cubs and hounds inside during cub hunting.

JINK: A sharp, almost right angled turn by a hunted animal, made to throw off its pursuers.

LIFT: To take hounds from the point where they have lost the scent quickly forward without waiting to cast again. One of the practices that speeded up hunting in the early days of the nineteenth century was lifting. When the huntsman thought the fox had gone on far ahead, he took hounds off the scent and then went towards where the fox had gone. Purists objected that lifting stopped hounds hunting for themselves. But it made hunting much faster. And more exciting. But if lifting was practised too much it could ruin the pack.

MASK: The head of the fox. Can also use the word pate.

OWN: Hounds are said to own the line when they pick up a scent.

PUSS: Hunting term for a hare.

RATE: To reprimand a hound.

RIOT: When hounds hunt any scent but that of the fox they are said to be running riot.

SCORING: Hounds are said to be scoring to cry when the scent is strong and every hound in the pack is speaking to it.

SINKING: When a hunted fox shows signs of being overtaken.

SKIRTER: A hound that runs wide of the pack and cuts corners rather than following the exact line of the fox.

SMEUSE: Gaps in hedges, fences or undergrowth, that a particular animal will habitually use.

STREAMING: Hounds running like flock of pigeons.

TALLY-HO: The cheer announcing that the fox is viewed emerging from a covert, but that he has headed back into the covert.

TICKLISH SCENT: One that varies or is uncertain.

TRENCHER-FED: Hounds kept not at a single kennels but at individual supporters' homes.

WARE: A huntsman's call to reprimand hounds. e.g 'Ware Sheep!'

WHO-HOOP: The cheer announcing the death of the fox.

A RESPECTABLE APPEARANCE IN THE PROVINCIALS

NIMROD was a journalist called Charles James Apperley, who chronicled the hunting of the 1820s. Rugby-educated Apperley was a hard riding sportsman who after a spell as a Dragoons officer, opted for a life of hunting in Leicestershire from an establishment paid for by his rich wife, daughter of a Welsh landowner.

But Apperley's wife left him and the money dried up. Much to his alarm, he was forced to find work. He tried horse-dealing but was conscious that this was not a gentleman's occupation. He turned to writing. He was a good writer and he persuaded Mr Pittman, proprietor of the *Sporting Magazine*, to give him a job.

Nimrod's Hunting Tours appeared in 1822. Apperley's opening lines were a witty discourse on his favourite county: 'Leicestershire, desirable as it is, has two great disadvantages; first, the crowd in the field; and secondly, it spoils a man for any other country, on which account no poor man should ever go near it. On the other hand its advantages are innumerable. It is the only country in the world that appears to have been intended for fox-hunting...The flower of our English youth also (of those at least worth looking at) have always been to be seen there, and a winter in Leicestershire has ever been found to be, to those who are entitled

to it, the passe-partout that leads to the best society in the world...Leicestershire may justly be denominated the Montpelier of hunting countries: in the eye of a sportsman it is the Vale of Cashmere...'.

The readers loved it. Nimrod's gossipy pieces on hunting squires and aristocrats trebled the magazine's circulation. Grateful Mr. Pittman shelled out for a string horses and paid £20 per page (£1500 today). Apperley was an intrepid social climber so it was no hardship to spend the season in England's great houses being entertained by the nobility keen to get their names – and their horses' and daughters' names, in that order – in his pages.

Apperley became a celebrity in Regency England. But smart packs like his beloved Quorn were out of his league financially. He remarked with surprising candour, 'A man like me with five hunters and a hack makes a very respectable appearance in the Provincials, but he has no business in Leicestershire'.

Short of being shot at, Apperley said that the greatest trial of nerve was putting a blown horse at a stiff timber fence in the afternoon. 'A report is flying about that one of the field is badly hurt, and something is heard of a collar-bone being broken, others say that it is a leg; but the pace is too good to inquire. A cracking of rails is now heard, and one gentleman's horse is to be seen resting, nearly balanced, across one of them, his rider being on his back in the ditch, which is on the landing side.'

He told the story of Mr Stanhope who fell on a Friday and went out with the Atherstone on a Monday with his arm in a sling. He fell again, was knocked out, but was up riding again by Thursday when he fell again at an impossibly high rail. The doctor diagnosed two broken ribs and a collapsed breastbone but otherwise

nothing serious. Nimrod remarked that Mr Stanhope was 'not a bad sort of man to breed from'.

Nimrod's reign ended with the death of his patron Mr. Pittman in 1828. The magazine's new proprietors were unimpressed by Apperley's ludicrous expenses and sued him for money advanced. To avoid debtor's prison, Apperley was forced to flee to Calais where he continued writing. When his finances allowed it he returned to England, dying in London in 1843.

FAITH AND NERVE

THE LATE NINETEENTH CENTURY American sporting writer Caspar Whitney was impressed by the bravery of the English foxhunter. The country back home in Long Island might have been dotted with terrifyingly huge post and rail jumps, but nothing could have prepared him for Leicestershire.

'It is not that the average jumps in England are so high or so stout so much as it is in the concealment of their true nature,' Whitney wrote in his 1894 book *Sporting Pilgrimage*. 'It is easy enough to pop over a bank with a hedge on top of it, but when that bank and hedge have a ditch on the take-off side, and in mid-air you get the first intimation of a yawning drain on the landing side also, you begin to appreciate some of the difficulties that make staying with the hounds no boy's play. When you have dropped into a "bottom", with its rotten and overhanging bank, and stayed there long enough to see the last of a straggling field go past you, you realise that all hunting in Leicestershire is not smooth going over velvety turf; and when you come, finally, to the terrific "oxers" and the staked-and-bound hedges, with timber on both sides, that are to be found in the Pytchley country, you conclude there is just as stiff jumping in England as the tallest and stoutest post-and-rails of Long Island.'

LARGE ENOUGH TO BE A SECOND HORSE

'SIZE IN A FOXHOUND is a matter which is frequently under discussion. The massively-built hound with immense bone, almost large enough to be used as a second horse and as cumbersome as an elephant, has now mercifully disappeared, and in its place has come a better balanced, more active, harder-wearing, and certainly more sightly animal…At puppy shows one often sees a well-made symmetrical young hound whose conformation leaves nothing to be desired; but when it is suggested that it be shown at Peterborough, one's inevitable reaction is "too small". There is no doubt that a certain standard of size and substance should be retained and both are dangerously easy to lose. A middle course is probably the safest one to steer and a kennel whose hounds are neither too large to go through thick brambles and undergrowth nor too small to negotiate the obstacles indigenous to the country, is obviously on the right track.'

Daphne Moore, The Book Of The Foxhound, *published by J. A. Allen, 1964*

Daphne Moore, born 1910, is regarded by many in the hunting community as the leading twentieth century authority on the foxhound.

Daughter of a Tewkesbury auctioneer, Daphne claimed to have spent a staggering 700 days foxhunting and 648 days otter-hunting in the decade leading up to the Second World War. After the war Daphne became *Horse & Hound's* correspondent on hounds and hound pedigrees and joined the Beaufort as an 'unofficial terrier woman'. She won the patronage of the Duke of Beaufort and took on the task of keeping His Grace's hound breeding pedigrees and entering his hounds for shows. She lived in a cottage next to Badminton.

Daphne followed the Beaufort on a large black ladies bicycle. She adored to hear hounds singing in kennel. She wrote, 'I have heard them at Badminton, chiming in tune with the church bells on a Sunday evening, or raising a paean of praise before dawn on a cubhunting morning'. She died unmarried in 2004 aged 94.

SNOW HUNTING

On founding the Hambledon Hunt in 1800, Mr Thomas Butler declared that one of the rules of the hunt should be that: 'No weather should stop hounds from going to the meet unless the snow should be one foot deep at the kennel door.'

HUNT CLASS

The thirty Royal Navy Hunt Class Type 1 destroyers of the Second World War:

Atherstone, Avon Vale, Badsworth, Berkeley, Blankney, Blencathra, Brocklesby, Cattistock, Cleveland, Cotswold, Croome, Cottesmore, Eglinton, Farndale, Fernie, Garth, Grove, Hamilton, Holderness, Lamerton, Limbourne, Mendip, Meynell, Puckeridge, Pytchley, Quantock, Quorn, Southdown, Tynedale, Whaddon

• The first Hunt Class vessels, named after British fox hunts, were ordered early in 1939. The class saw extensive service in the Second World War, particularly on the British East Coast and Mediterranean convoys.

• On the seabed of the Mediterranean off Gibraltar the hunt class destroyer HMS *Puckeridge* lies with most of her crew, three Lionel Edwards prints of the Puckeridge hounds, which adorned the officers' mess, and a silver hunting horn, a gift from the Masters of the hunt. When *Puckeridge* was torpedoed by a German U-boat in September, 1943, the hunt set up a committee to raise money to replace her. In six weeks the appeal had raised enough not only to replace HMS *Puckeridge* but to build an additional *three* destroyers. If only it was as easy to raise hunt funds these days. Nineteen other hunt class ships were lost during the war. Others were scrapped or sold off. HMS *Cottesmore* ended up in the Egyptian navy and HMS *Oakley* went to the reformed German navy where she was renamed *Gneisenau*.

• Today's Royal Navy Hunt Class consists of eight mine countermeasure ships with GRP hulls. They are *Atherstone, Cattistock, Brocklesby, Ledbury, Chiddingfold, Quorn, Hurworth, Middleton*. Considering the last Labour Government's anti-hunting stance, it is surprising that these ships were not renamed after football clubs.

THE MASTER IS GOD

Some basic tips for the (pre-Ban!) novice:

1. Never crack your whip.
2. Never flick at a hound with your whip.
3. Remember that your Hunt has not bought a monopoly of the roads and lanes.
4. Remember that the Hunt only crosses the farmers' land by their courtesy.
5. Remember that you are not the only person out hunting.
6. Obey the Master's wishes immediately and implicitly.
7. When hounds are drawing keep behind and as close to the Field Master as you can get.
8. When hounds go away with a fox never cut off the tail hounds from the main body.
9. Do not press on hounds at any time, especially during the early stages of a hunt.
10. Never ride between the huntsman and his hounds.
11. Stand still and keep quiet when hounds check.
12. When you meet hounds always turn your horse's head towards them.
13. If your horse kicks put a red ribbon on its tail, but do not trust to that alone to keep you out of trouble.
14. Learn to open and catch gates. Every field in England has at least one gate to it.
15. If someone dismounts to open a gate no one must go beyond him until he is on his horse again.
16. Concentration is essential if you want to keep with hounds.
17. A sound take-off is the first esssential when selecting your place at a fence.
18. A black, strong-looking fence is much safer than a weak, straggly one.

From The Young Foxhunter *by David Brock MFH of the East Sussex, A and C Black, 1936*

• David Brock described how to make the perfect hunting sandwich: 'Hunting sandwiches differ from all other sandwiches in that they are eaten under vastly more rigorous conditions, and they should be prepared with that in view. They should be so cut, formed and packed that they can be enjoyed even though eaten upon the back of a runaway mustang, in a hurricane of wind and cold rain, by a man who has recently broken his right wrist.'

DEVILISH EXCITEMENT

FATHER OF THE REVOLUTION Frederick Engels was famous for hunting regularly with the Cheshire during the 1850s.

Engels, co-author of the Communist Manifesto with Karl Marx, found the hunt's educated, upper class company such as the Marquis of Grosvenor and Earl of Crewe a welcome diversion from the proletariat at his family's Manchester cotton factory where he worked.

Engels was full of humbug. He dressed up hunting with left-wing justifications, claiming that come the revolution his experiences in the field would enable him to lead cavalry charges against the capitalists.

Engels loved hunting. After a particularly good day he wrote to Marx, 'On Saturday I went out fox-hunting – seven hours in the saddle. That sort of thing always keeps me in a state of devilish excitement for several days; it's the greatest physical pleasure I know.'

ODE TO AN ADMIRAL

Bold Tar! who for so many winters
Has knocked our five-bar gates to splinters
We this memorial beg to send,
In hopes you will our fences mend.
We love to see you stick to hounds,
For your ambition knows no bounds:
And be our fences oak or ash,
Your horses drive them all to smash.
You ride, begirt with scarlet spencer,
On many a high-bred, splendid fencer.
But, if you'll hold them more in hand,
They'll higher jump at your command.

*This anonymous poem was dedicated to nineteenth century
Admiral Henry Micklethwait, R.N., who hunted in Norfolk.*

BUTTERFLIES

Research by the Game and Wildlife Conservation Trust proves that rare
butterflies occur more frequently in woodland managed for hunting.

STRONG AND SILENT

'Horses are like husbands: they are the strong silent ones and
dearly love to think they have their own way.' Lady Apsley (1895–
1966). The formidable Violet Apsley was a Conservative MP and
keen horsewoman who wrote several books about hunting. She
was MFH of the VWH from 1946 to 1956 when she broke her
back in a hunting accident. She spent her remaining years in a
wheelchair. Lady Apsley was not the most perceptive of ladies.
During a campaigning trip to Tyneside she astonished even fellow
Tories when she suggested to some out of work miners that they
ought to go hunting. Their reply was none too polite.

PRECEDENCE

'The fox takes precedence of *all* from the cover;
The horse is an animal properly bred
After the pack to be ridden, not over,
Good hounds are not rear'd to be knocked on the head.'

From A Word 'Ere We Start, *by nineteenth century Cheshire landowner Rowland Edgerton-Warburton (1804-1891). Edgerton Warburton was President of the Tarporley Hunt Club and published many poems, mostly about hunting. His old Eton friend, the Liberal politician Lord Halifax, described him as 'a perfect combination: a good churchman, a good landlord, a keen sportsman, and a man of literary tastes'.*

BRITISH DASH

Despite being soundly thrashed at the Battle of Waterloo, Napoleon's commanders were disparaging about British officers. Marshal Excelmann, head of Bonaparte's 2nd Cavalry Corps, wrote to an English friend, 'Your British horses are the finest in the world, and your men ride better than any Continental soldiers...but the great deficiency is in your officers: the British cavalry officer seems to be impressed with the conviction that he can dash and ride over everything; as if the art of war were precisely the same as that of fox-hunting.'

USELESS INFORMATION

The Tiverton Foxhounds are the only hunt to have been hunted by a man who subsequently became Chancellor of the Exchequer – Derek Heathcoat Amory, who came to the post in 1958 under Prime Minster Harold Macmillan.

CLEVER OLD HUNTER

'When commencing to hunt, the beginner should make a start on a clever old hunter that knows its business thoroughly and can take care both of itself and its rider, for the latter cannot possibly understand at first how each description of fence requires to be done, and he will learn much from such a steed. It will not matter if it is rather a screw, so long as it is sound enough to do its share of the partnership, the main thing being that it is thoroughly accomplished and easy to ride, so that the pupil may have no difficulty in following where he sees other people go. It is time enough to get on to a raw, or difficult, horse when knowledge has come of what to do and how to do it; then it is necessary to ride more difficult horses, for no one ever became a really fine horseman by only riding well-made hunters.'

Meysey-Thompson was an Army bod who hunted all his life from the age of nineteen when he bought his first horse as a humble subaltern in the Rifle Brigade. As a beginner he had little money to spend on foxhunting. 'I did not therefore venture on the expense of a groom, but essayed to manage for the horse myself, with the assistance of my soldier servant, whose only qualification for the task was that he had been in the Camel Corps in the Indian Mutiny. I found the one of us knew about as much, or rather as little, as the other. However, we managed somehow, and the pleasure I got out of my horse was immense.'

Colonel Richard Meysey-Thompson,
A Hunting Catechism, *1907*

STAY ON TOP

'Ponies on non-hunting days are usually good natured enough to stand quietly beside a child who has fallen off, and let him remount. But take a pony and child out behind a pack of hounds, and the child shares the pony's company just as long as he stays on top.'

Thriller writer and keen hunting man Dick Francis

GAY AND CHEERFUL

'The cut and colour of a foxhunter's coat are matter of taste, opinion, or profession; scarlet has been ever considered the most appropriate, as patronised by royalty some centuries ago, and it certainly gives a gay and cheerful aspect to the hunting-field. Green is also assigned to the hunting of deer and hares; but as it has been said that a good horse cannot be of a bad colour, a good rider is certain to make himself conspicuous in whatever cloth he may appear; and we have remarked that a "gentleman in black" can hold his own across country, and compete with his brothers in brighter hues.'

From The Science of Foxhunting and Management of the Kennel, *KnightleyWilliam Horlock, 1868*

• The colour of hunt coats can be impossibly complicated to outsiders. For example, the Beaufort's huntsman and whippers-in wear green, the colour of the Beaufort family livery, while subscribers wear blue and buff. The Berkeley wear yellow and the Heythrop's huntsman wears green because part of Heythrop country was formerly part of the Beaufort. The Pytchley do not wear red coats but wear crimson coats made of what is known as Padua red; Pytchley Masters wear a white collar, originally worn to protect the coat from a powdered wig. During the eighteenth century many foxhunting squires switched to wearing the green coats of the Tory Party. But by the early nineteenth century red was back in fashion thanks to the Duke of Wellington's officers who hunted in regimental scarlet. After Waterloo red became recognised as the colour of foxhunting, although farmers traditionally wore black.

HOOTIN'

ALL COLONIAL GOVERNORS of British colonies until the Second World War listed fishing as their recreation in *Who's Who*. Most of them listed hunting and shooting as well. In 1946, Sir Frederick Burrows, former president of the National Union of Railwaymen who in 1946 was appointed Governor of Bengal by a Labour Government, put down his hobbies as 'shuntin', hootin' and whistlin''.

MEYNELLIAN SCIENCE

The founding father of English foxhunting was Hugo Meynell, founder of the Quorn who began hunting hounds from his Leicestershire seat Quorn Hall in 1753. He developed the science of hunting the fox at speed in the open, made possible by the clearance of forests and the enclosure of land.

Meynell transformed hunting from just another method of vermin control into the premier country sport. He bred a pack capable of keeping up with a fast running fox at midday. With its fenced grassland and strong scent, Meynell's Quorn became the heart of English hunting. In what became known as the 'Meynellian Science', Meynell divided his pack into two, consisting of old and young hounds. The big woods were hunted by the young pack two days a week, whilst the good country was kept for the experienced hounds. Meynell loved his hounds. On returning from hunting he would always see them fed first before sitting down to dinner himself.

Meynell owned little land and hunted by invitation. He was no great rider and and saw his horse as just a method of conveying him to hounds. A friend described him as 'A regular little dumpling on horseback'.

In the 1790s Meynell hunted three days a week, killing up to ninety-two foxes a year. He hated hard riding and was known for his sarcastic put downs. When someone rode over the scent and then insisted he was in the right, Meynell would reply, 'You may be perfectly right, sir, and I quite wrong, but there is gross ignorance on one side or the other'.

Meynell was the first Master to establish order and discipline in the hunting field. He hated it if someone positioned himself at the covertside where the fox was expected to break and subsequently headed the fox. He had an unusual way of dealing with jealous riders. Instead of chastising the culprit, Meynell would scold his whipper-in instead in the hope that the offender would hear: 'You damned fool! Come away instantly, spoiling the sport of the whole field!'

Much to Meynell's dismay, by the end of his mastership the Quorn was being taken over by young bloods determined to ride as fast as they could and to hell with hounds. Meynell hated fast riding. After listening to some young Quorn men boasting of their exploits at the end the day, he murmured, 'I wonder where you find all these great places to leap – I never come across them'.

Meynell died in 1808 aged seventy-four.

• Hugo Meynell carried a hip flask containing an alcoholic beverage known as tincture of rhubarb. 'A nasty drink to which he was much addicted,' remarked a friend.

LOVE LETTER

HUNTING gained a more formal footing in 1856 with the creation of the Masters of Hounds Committee, which met at Boodles Club in London.

It will come as no great surprise to learn that this tribunal was founded partly as a result of a sexual indiscretion by a Master of Foxhounds. The Master of the Cheshire, Captain Arthur Mainwaring, was discovered to have written a love letter to a married woman with whom he was conducting an illicit liaison. When the Cheshire members asked him to resign, Mainwaring refused. The landowners of Cheshire were outraged and banned him from their coverts. Subscribers withheld their subs. The Master and his opponents were ordered before the committee. The committee judged that Mainwaring was in the wrong and told him to quit. He went quietly.

The Boodles Committee, as it became known, arbitrated in quarrels between neighbouring packs, mainly boundary disputes. Their word became law in the hunting community, though farmers were unimpressed to hear disputes being referred to a London club and were even crosser when they were unable to meet Mr Boodle in person.

In 1881 the hunting committee members left Boodles after a dispute whereupon the Duke of Beaufort invited MFHs throughout the country to form the Master of Foxhounds Association which is the sport's governing body today.

UNWRITTEN LAWS

A feud between two brothers, George and Henry Wyndham, erupted into one of the biggest spats in foxhunting. Illegitimate sons of Lord Egremont, the pair were Masters of different packs of foxhounds hunting in Sussex.

Trouble began in 1837 when George inherited the family seat Petworth House and started hunting on ground that was also being hunted by Henry.

Henry was outraged. A snarling correspondence ensued. The argument became public. Opinion was divided. Henry argued that George had broken unwritten laws of foxhunting by poaching on his territory. The brothers appealed to three peers, also MFHs, who were asked to rule. M'lords decided that since Henry had hunted the ground first he had a right to remain there. In revenge, George ordered his staff to slaughter every fox on the place leaving Henry nothing to hunt. Deprived of his sport, Henry had a nervous breakdown and retired to Cumberland. With nobody in his way, George continued to hunt his ground, establishing what was to become the Leconfield Hunt. Which proves the rule that when under pressure Masters of Foxhounds do exactly as they please.

GAMEKEEPER'S CON

'The following is a system which has been known to be adopted by keepers who are determined enemies to foxes, and who wish their masters to believe, not only that they are very attentive to their duty, but that foxes do much more harm than they really do. The keeper shoots a hen pheasant, and having cut it into several pieces he lays the feathers, which are bloody, about the covert, probably in twenty different places. Shortly afterwards he begs his master to go and see the damage the fox has done. Having shown such convincing proof, he often gains permission to kill the fox'.

From The Life Of A Fox Written By Himself And Extracts From The Diary Of A Huntsman, *by Thomas Smith, 1843*

- Vulpicide: 'The action of killing a fox otherwise than hunting by hounds'.

From Oxford English Dictionary

FOX FOOD

Here is TV personality and hunt supporter Clarissa Dickson Wright's recipe for Fox Casserole. Apparently fox is a bit like veal, but a lot chewier.

1. Catch your fox.
2. Skin and gut it.
3. Hang the fox in running water for three days.
4. Cook with garlic, onion and tomato, as if you were cooking rabbit the Italian way: lay in a dish, cover, and stew for about an hour and a half.
5. Cut the fox into halves, not quarters.
6. Serve with chestnut pasta; drink with a good Italian wine.

Clarissa points out that fox is the closest that many oriental races, such as Thais, can get to dog and remain legal. Manchester is the main market for exporting fox to Thailand.

- After a hard day's hunting in the 1790s, the 2nd Duke of Northumberland's hounds eventually caught their fox. The Duke was so delighted that he had the creature's head devilled and ate it for dinner. It was served with macaroni. Northumberland was the richest man in England and known for his bad temper, presumably not helped by eating fox.

PRIORITIES

ON HIS DEATHBED, MR NICHOLAS PARRY, a nineteenth century Master of the Puckeridge, was asked: 'If you could live your life over again, what would you do different?'

He replied, 'I should put in a few more days before Christmas.'

PERCEPTION

WRITER JILLY COOPER on 'antis': 'Hunting is popularly seen as an upper-class sport, practised by the rich and seemingly arrogant. It would be more honest to call the dissenters the Anti-Blue-Blood-Sports Brigade.'

DIFFICULT TO FIND

'The highest praise that can be given to a huntsman is for a fool to say: "We had a great run, and killed our fox; as for the huntsman, he might have been in bed". A huntsman's first boast should be that all his hounds required was to be taken to the covert-side and taken home again. His greatest disgrace is, first, to have his hounds squandered all over the country, and to leave them out; second, to be unable to get them out of a wood; third, not to know to a yard where he lost his fox – if properly managed, the hounds will always tell it to him.'

Lord Henry Bentinck (1804–1870).

• Lord Henry was a Member of Parliament and keen hunting man who wrote a series of letters on handling hounds. The fourth son of the 4th Duke of Portland, he played a significant part in establishing Disraeli as leader of the Conservative party. It is said that having done so, he proceeded to devote his life to hunting in the winter (he was Master of the Burton, in Lincolnshire), deer stalking in the autumn (he perfected his aim in the summer by practising with a pea-shooter) and playing whist in the summer. He was the finest whist player in Europe and invented the call for trumps known as Blue Peter.

Henry excelled at hunting. A friend remarked that he had 'the best brain that was ever given to hounds'. He dressed in black in the field and was often mistaken for a preacher.

While Master of the Burton Henry hunted six days a week, riding upwards of thirty miles to meets from his home at Welbeck Abbey in Nottinghamshire. In winter he never saw Welbeck by daylight, except on Sundays which he spent throwing balls to young hounds. A fellow master once said to him, 'Six days a week hunting is too much for any man'. Bentinck replied, 'When the church is abolished, there will be no obstacle to hunting seven'.

Lord Henry died at a friend's estate in Lincolnshire, on 31 December 1870. The cause of death was heart failure following an otherwise satisfactory day's shooting.

• Lord Henry Bentinck's brother Lord George Bentinck was also a Conservative MP and the last man to wear hunting red in the House of Commons. He would arrive in the house from hunting in Hampshire wearing a white great-coat over his hunting coat. In 1854 Bentinck came to prominence by supporting Conservative leader Benjamin Disraeli in opposing Prime Minister Robert Peel's repeal of the Corn Laws. His resentment towards Peel galvanised him so much that having been frequently absent from the Commons for years, he gave up hunting and devoted his life to politics.

• The finest horseman of the Bentinck family was older brother William, later 5th Duke of Portland. He was so obsessed by riding that he contructed a gigantic riding school at his Nottinghamshire family seat Welbeck Abbey. William built a labyrinth of underground rooms beneath Welbeck and became a recluse. He only ventured outside in utmost secrecy, dressed in a brace of overcoats and hiding behind an umbrella.

DEPARTED HUNTING GLORY

HUNTING IN IRELAND disintegrated in 1881 as the peasantry took out their anger on landowners during the Land War. When English landlords evicted tenants for non-payment of rent, locals found the most effective retaliation was to target hunts. Hounds and foxes were poisoned; coverts and kennels burned. Those at meets risked stoning by the angry mob.

During the 1881–2 season the English foxhunters quit Ireland.

Baily's Sporting Magazine blamed the uprising on American agitators, declaring: 'Ah! shade of departed hunting glory, blood-bedewed, disgraced Ireland. Why have you driven out from amongst you the residents, the well-wishers, the sportsmen, and their money, and have fallen into the trap that the Irish-Americans have laid for you, baited with dollars drawn from the pockets of your miserable emigrants?'

Ironically, several Irish packs were sold to America. The Marquess of Waterford fled to England and continued his sport in Gloucestershire. Likewise Lord Cloncurry debunked to England. In *Baily's* words, Ireland was 'no longer the green isle beloved of sportsmen' and the early 1880s saw much of the country unhunted.

OLD FAVOURITE

'The English country gentleman galloping after a fox – the unspeakable in full pursuit of the uneatable'.
Oscar Wilde.

This well-worn quote appears in Wilde's 1893 play *A Woman Of No Importance,* one of his weaker works. In usual Wilde fashion the play deals with upper class secrets. It involves a peer who discovers that the young man he has employed as a secretary is in fact his illegitimate son. The 'unspeakable' quote appears early on when the characters Lady Caroline, Mr Kelvil MP, Mrs Allonby, and Lord Illingworth are discussing the merits of entertainment for the working classes…

LADY CAROLINE. I am not at all in favour of amusements for the poor, Jane. Blankets and coals are sufficient. There is too much love of pleasure amongst the upper classes as it is. Health is what we want in modern life. The tone is not healthy, not healthy at all.

KELVIL. You are quite right, Lady Caroline.

LADY CAROLINE. I believe I am usually right.

MRS ALLONBY. Horrid word 'health'.

LORD ILLINGWORTH. Silliest word in our language, and one knows so well the popular idea of health. The English country gentleman galloping after a fox – the unspeakable in full pursuit of the uneatable.

KELVIL. May I ask, Lord Illingworth, if you regard the House of Lords as a better institution than the House of Commons?

LORD ILLINGWORTH. A much better institution, of course. We in the House of Lords are never in touch with public opinion. That makes us a civilised body.

• Tony Blair repeated Wilde's quote during his 1999 Labour Party conference speech when he described the Conservatives as 'the party of foxhunting, Pinochet and hereditary peers – the uneatable, the unspeakable and the unelectable'. Blair soon regretted this attack on foxhunting. In private he wasn't bothered by hunting. Cherie was always said to be the big anti in the family, although she denied it in her autobiography. Tony wished later that the issue would go away. But it did not. Having taken a £100,000 donation to the Labour Party from International Fund for Animal Welfare (IFAW), Blair felt committed to squandering taxpayers' millions on an absurd law, which ironically was to become the stuff of an Oscar Wilde play.

• It should be noted that in the past IFAW has made donations to both the Liberal Democrats and the Conservatives, though these amounts were thought to be smaller than the sums given to Labour.

DON'T MENTION THE PLOUGH

IN COMMON with most Victorian sporting writers, Charles Bindley was obsessed with class and doing the right thing on the hunting field. Bindley wrote under the pseudonym Harry Hieover and was described as writing 'under the same exhilaration of spirits as he might have felt when going across country'.

Here Hiover offers some killer lines to the commoner expecting to become pally with dukes simply by going hunting with them:

'I am quite aware that any stranger making his first appearance at a meet of our aristocratic hunts would find many an eye-glass levelled at him, and it would be certain to be detected to what class he belonged ; but if it was known he was a plain farmer…who had merely come to treat himself with a week with the Quorn, without any intention of being considered as one of them, the men he would meet there would be the last in the world to mention a plough in his presence. Nay, they would be very likely to give him an invite, and if he acted his natural part, would treat him as, and consider him, a trump. But one attempt at equality his fate is sealed; aristocracy will often welcome a man of another grade as being with them, but he must not attempt to be one of them.'

NO SHAME

'Foxhunting is now become the amusement of gentlemen: nor need any gentleman be ashamed of it'. Georgian hunting writer Peter Beckford.

Until the mid-eighteenth century foxhunting was considered vulgar. Posh people hunted stags; to describe someone as a 'foxhunter' was to call them an oik.

Beckord (1740–1810), linguist, wit, and gentleman, kept hounds in Dorset and lived on an inherited West Indian fortune. It has been said that what Izaak Walton is to angling, Beckford is to foxhunting. He was a cultivated enlightenment dandy, well travelled and highly educated. He was said to 'bag a fox in Greek, find a hare in Latin, inspect his kennels in Italian, and direct the economy of his stables in exquisite French'.

Beckford set out to give foxhunting a mystique. The publication of *Thoughts On Hunting*

in 1781 made him a minor celebrity with sentences such as: 'You will…find pleasure in the breeding of hounds, in which expectation is never completely satified, and it is on the sagacious management of this business that all your success will depend'.

Beckford regarded hunting as 'the soul of country life'. He argued that gentlemen would not be tempted by the debaucheries of London if hunting was well established in the countryside. This would benefit all rural society. Foxhunting trained men for war. Or as he put it: 'It prevents our young men from growing effeminate in Bond Street'.

• Beckford warned that the traditional cure to stop a hound worrying sheep by tying it to an old ram who would kick it around a bit, did not always work as intended. Beckford told the story of a friend who put the largest ram he could find into his kennel with a couple of erring hounds. The ram was a vicious sod. 'Egad! There is a not a dog dares look him in the face', Beckford's friend boasted. But wasn't he worried that the hounds might be hurt? 'No. Damn them! They deserve it. Let them suffer.' A few hours later Beckford and his friend returned to the kennel. Opening the door, they could see the hounds in a corner sound asleep. There was no sign of the ram. Beckford explained, 'The ram had been entirely eaten up. The hounds, having filled their bellies, were retired to rest.'

IPI KAI YAY

During operations in 1937 on the Northwest Frontier in Waziristan against the Fakir of Ipi the British Army amused itself with a drag hunt. The Master was Brigadier George Young, polo player and foxhunter, who later organised the mule trains in Burma during World War II. Young endeared himself to his men when he organised a point to point. A squadron of armoured cars was deployed around the course in order to discourage snipers.

HOUNDS AHEAD

ONE OF THE THE WORLD'S LONGEST-SERVING MFHs is Nancy Penn Smith Hannum who led Mr Stewart's Cheshire Foxhounds, in the country of Unionville, Pennsylvania, continuously for fifty-eight years from 1948 to 2006.

The pack was founded in 1912 by Mrs Hannum's step-father. Unionville looks as if it has been designed for hunting. The area has more post and rail fence per capita than anywhere else in the United State and road crossings are dotted with signs announcing 'Horses and Hounds Ahead'.

Throughout her life Mrs Hannum has worked with more than 1,000 hounds since she arrived with her beagles at a boarding school in Virginia aged thirteen. Of Unionville, she says, 'This place is God's heaven. We used to go to Leicestershire, England, and everyone would "ooh" and "aah". But I couldn't wait to come home.'

WHERE ONE IS CARELESS OF ONE'S PURSE

THE WORLD'S HUNTING EPICENTRE is Melton Mowbray, the Leicestershire market town bordered by some of England's greatest packs: The Quorn, Cottesmore, Pytchley, and Belvoir.

The first hunting visitor to arrive in Melton was Durham colliery owner William Lambton in around 1800. Lambton, a shy man, was exasperated with the noisy hunting set in Loughborough, home to Hugo Meynell's Quorn. So he fled down the road to Melton, rented a house and stabled his hunters there.

Lambton had no idea that he had started England's longest running house party. The next season he was joined by M'Lords Forester and Delamere, who took a house in Burton Street and named it The Old Club. The house had only four bedrooms so competition for membership was fierce. The Prince Regent became a regular guest.

During the golden age of hunting, 1810 to 1830, up to 300 hunters were stabled in Melton with owners hunting six days a week. The Old Club's social activities were legend. There was cock fighting, whoring and gambling. After dinner horses were bid for over bottles of claret. The next morning saw bewildered faces on the grooms as horses changed stables.

More clubs were started such as the New Club, launched by Lord Alvanley. People spent huge sums on hunters. It was considered smart not to know how many horses were in your stables. Many owned up to twenty hunters each and some like the Earl of Plymouth had many more than that. Journalist Adam Waldie commeted in 1833: 'Melton is one of the places in the world where one is most careless of one's purse and person and where the one and the other are sacrificed with the greatest zest.'

Until women began hunting properly in the mid 1800s, life in Melton was dull for them. The men departed at 6 am and didn't return until 6 pm. Nor was the town a fit place for ladies. Prostitutes were numerous. At night, the girls would tap on the clubs' windows, and the men would sneak out into the night for a spot of monkey business in an alleyway.

By the end of the nineteenth century it is said that the town was seeing up to 50,000 sporting visitors a year. Meltonians were a hearty bunch. Hunting boxes could be primitive. By the 1870s there were still no bathrooms, water was pumped from wells and there was no electrcity. The rooms were tiny. But coal was plentiful and there were dozens of servants.

Late nineteenth century Melton regular Lady Augusta Fane claimed that despite the deprivations people were warm and comfortable. 'Many preferred their winter quarters at Melton to their large rambling country houses. I sometimes wonder if we were not better off with a bath in one's bedroom before a roaring fire, with relays of cans of boiling water, which avoided the necessity of walking down passages to a bathroom and having to wait one's turn for the bath, whilst the water runs cold.'

You had to be rich to hunt in Leicestershire. Merchants saw you coming. Oats and hay were more expensive in Melton than anywhere else in Britain. But the superb sport more than made up for the expense. The soil was highly favourable to scent and much of the land was given over to grazing with little under plough. There were few large woods. Coverts were small and perfect for foxhunting.

• When Queen Victoria visited Melton in 1843 she was greeted at the entrance of the town with a trumphal arch covered with evergreen and topped off with a line of stuffed foxes.

• From about 1850s Victorian morality placed a temporary stranglehold on Melton's gambling and drinking. The rollicking hunt ball was abandoned and replaced by an event called The Primrose Ball. This was a semi-political affair started by Colchester do-gooder MP Sir Herbert Mackworth Praed. A participant described it as 'a tiresome dance'. Mackworth Praed, founder of Melton's working men's club, rode hard and endured frequent bad falls. He was described as 'very good looking and exceedingly fond of the ladies'. Evidently he had a problem making decisions of the heart – he died a bachelor at the age of eighty-two.

• By 1850 the Melton Mowbray Old Club had fizzled out. The building became a private house. In the 1880s it was bought by baronet Sir Beaumont Dixie and his wife Lady Florence Dixie, sister of the Marquis of Queensbury. Much to the alarm of the parson who lived next door, Lady Florence, an early feminist and war correspondent, kept a jaguar in the garden. She had brought the beast home from Africa. As well as hunting, Florence loved football and in 1895 became President of the British Ladies' Football Club.

• Best bet made at Melton was during the latter half of the nineteenth century by a fellow called Peter Flower, who wagered that he could ride a horse up the staircase to the first floor of the hunting lodge he shared with his two brothers. Flower galloped his huge bay up the stairs to the landing. All very good. But nothing would induce the creature to come down again. This was after dinner on a Saturday night. The horse stayed there all day Sunday. It was not until Monday morning that workmen were available to construct a platform so that the horse could be lowered to the ground by ropes. The hunter was subsequently sold to Irish peer Lord Annaly who renamed him First Flight.

RULES

'He/she rides under both sets of rules.' An expression often heard in the racing world – but just as widely used on the hunting field – to describe a subscriber who is bisexual.

ONE HOBBY

Sir Richard Sutton, Master of the Quorn in the 1850s was so rich that he dispensed with the subscription and paid for the entire hunt himself. When a fellow member of the Quorn told him where to draw, he replied, 'Sir, I have only one hobby: it costs me £10,000 a year and I go where I like'.

FEARLESSNESS

'Hunting demands fearlessness…it was no accident that the fighter pilots in the Battle of Britain went into action against the German bombers to the cheer of "Tally Ho!" over the intercom…nor that the music which the German troops heard from the advancing British infantry in Normandy on D-day was the brave but gentle note of the hunting horn.'

Wilson Stephens, editor of The Field *during the 1960s*

SIBLING RIVALRY

A significant moment in the development of foxhunting arrived in 1809 with an action brought by the landowning Earl of Essex against his half brother the Hon. and Rev. William Capel, Master of the Old Berkeley.

Astonishing though it may seem today, until the early nineteenth century hunts had simply presumed a right to ride over anybody's land without permission on the pretext that they were in pursuit of vermin. This right had been confirmed in a court ruling of 1788 by Mr Justice Buller who declared that a hunter could pursue a fox across another man's land so long as he did not cause damage to fields or fences 'more than is absolutely necessary'. The Buller ruling was used by hunts to enter land as they pleased.

Lord Essex and his half-brother hated each other. In 1808 the sibling rivalry came to a head when Essex made a formal complaint to the Old Berkeley about damage being done on his land. The hunt failed to respond. A few months later Essex's keepers closed a gate to the hunt. In retaliation, dozens of riders deliberately broke through fences and entered his land. Essex brought an action for trespass and won his case. The Chief Justice Lord Ellenborough ruled that foxes were hunted for pleasure and 'those pleasures are to be taken only when there is the consent of those who are likely to be injured by them'.

Ellenborough's ruling had been done through gritted teeth. To demonstrate that he considered Essex was a pretty poor sport, the judge awarded him only one shilling damages. However, Essex was delighted that the Chief Justice had established the principle that farmers objecting to a hunt's activities could now sue for trespass. Far from hindering hunts, the ruling did the sport a power of good. It reinforced the fact that Masters needed the goodwill of landowners and farmers if they were to continue.

CONFUSED BY FISH

THE HAZARDS OF HUNTING near London were highlighted one day in the early 1700s when the the Essex Foxhounds were joined by a well-to-do fishmonger from Piccadilly. The fellow smelled so strongly that hounds were put off the scent and the day was cancelled. 'The whole country smelled of fish', Essex MFH Henry Conyers complained.

BIG GIRL

GREATEST ROYAL HUNTING LADY of them all was Queen Anne, who ruled from 1702 to 1714. Anne and her husband Prince George of Denmark were devoted to the sport and in their younger days spent much of their time riding with staghounds in Berkshire.

In middle-age Anne became so fat that she was forced to use a specially built chariot in order to follow her pack. She drove her vehicle all day, sometimes up to forty miles through specially-constructed rides. The writer Jonathan Swift attended one of these hunts. Anne captained her contraption like a maniac. 'The Queen drives like Jehu,' he noted.

Sadly, years of compulsive gorging forced Anne to abandon her beloved sport in her late fifties. A contemporary writer observed, 'Her health might perhaps have been longer preserved had she not eaten so much'.

BEST THING IN THE WORLD

'An aged clergyman, a very religious man, once declared that the best thing which this world afforded was a good run, the next best was a bad run, the next best a day with hounds on which you had no run. Many men who really love hunting will at once agree. And many who have not the taste for it will shrug their shoulders.'

The Spectator, *1902*

ONLY HAZY

For those of you who hate getting up on a wet hunting day…

No more the punctual groom shall shake
His master till they both awake,
To listen to the wind and rain
At six loud clattering on the pane,
And envy those who stretch and yawn
Careless of bleak December's dawn;
Or doze perchance some lie inventing
To shirk this famous day for scenting,
To get the inexorable groom,
And his damned candle from the room;
While gusts more strong and showers more thick,
Give him strange thoughts of shamming sick:
Till mindful of his former fame,
He combats drowsiness with shame;
Till (resolution gathering strength,
And Slumber from his limbs at length
Loosening the chains which bind the lazy)
He votes the morning only hazy.

From *Advice To Julia*, by Henry Luttrell, 1820. Luttrell (1768–1851) illegitimate son of the second Earl of Carhampton and a gardener's daughter, was a London poet who used his wit to climb into the top drawer of London society. Famous for his epigrams, Luttrell was one of those people who never seemed to make much money but managed, through connections such as the Duchess of Devonshire, to live remarkably well. His 'society epic' *Advice To Julia*, was described by a critic as 'full of well-bred facetiousness and sparkle'. It was reprinted three times.

Luttrell wrote some good lines on how you needed money
to hunt in Leicestershire:

'…at Melton all partakers
In hunting should be men of acres,
Or flush of money in the Stocks,
In order to suppress the fox'.

GHASTLY GILBERT

EARLY EIGHTEENTH CENTURY millionaire merchant Sir Gilbert Heathcote, universally disliked as a notoriously mean man despite being described as the 'richest commoner in England', was hunting on his Derbyshire estate when he saw his parson take a bad fall. 'You can lie where you are, sir,' Sir Gilbert brayed. 'You won't be wanted 'til next Sunday.'

• Until the middle of the nineteenth century, it was common for country parsons to give out the week's meet list in church. On the Yorkshire Wolds there was a tradition whereby a parson would give 5 shillings (25p) for every dead fox brought to the rectory gate. Down in the West Country a Victorian curate called the Rev. Mr Wright refused to feature the Athanasian Creed in his services, though repeatedly asked to do so by his parishioners. They complained to the Bishop, who ordered Mr. Wright to use it. The following Sunday the curate told his congregation, 'Next follows St Athanasius's Creed, either to be said or sung, and with God's leave I'll sing it'. Whereupon the choir commenced singing the words to a popular foxhunting-drinking song. The parishioners called a meeting and informed their curate that they would dispense with the Creed in future.

PARSON'S PAD

THE REV. DR PENNY, chaplain to the foxhunting mad 5th Duke of Beaufort at Badminton, had a doorbell pull to which was attached a fox's pad. The setting bore an inscription informing visitors that the pad was taken from the first fox killed by the Duke's pack of hounds.

• A bonkers Berkshire brandy merchant called Thomas Philips spent his life collecting fox pads, which he had cut off himself when in at the kill. His trophies were nailed to his stable doors. Philips died in 1787 at the age of sixty-seven. In his will he requested that he be placed in his coffin with a fox pad in each hand.

• In some hunting circles it was the fashion to stir the Christmas punch with a stuffed fox's pad. According to John B. Skinner, editor of the 1882 *American Sporting Magazine*, punch tasted much better when 'scented with reynard's foot'. Other drinks could also benefit from a dash of fox, wrote Skinner who had 'carried his ardour more than once so far as to immerse the foot of a fox recently killed in a bumper of port'.

FLYING

About the only historical family hunting connection of which this author can boast (and it is pretty obscure) is that my great, great, great, great Aunt Harriet Cludde married a Shropshire gent called William Lacon Childe, of Kinlet Park. Harriet's father-in-law, also named William, was known throughout late eighteenth-century England as our finest horseman. He was nicknamed The Flying Childe because of his daring on the hunting field. Childe is credited with inventing in 1780 the 'flying leap' – jumping out at a canter or gallop rather than from a standstill. Masters of fox hounds at that time hated such showy displays and complained that people like Childe were ruining hunting. They hunted only for the sake of riding and cared little about hounds. Legendary master Hugo Meynell grumbled that since Childe had brought the flying leap to Leicestershire he 'hadn't had a moment's peace'. He described Childe as going at a 'splitter-cockation pace'.

• Childe got his nickname from a racehorse called Flying Childers (born 1704) which is considered the world's first truly great thoroughbred. The horse, bred by a Colonel Leonard Childers from Doncaster and bought by the Duke of Devonshire, won every single race he entered. The Duke received endless offers for the animal, including one of the animal's weight in gold crowns. The horse is remembered to this day in a race at Doncaster called The Flying Childers Stakes.

HUNTING FROM A RAILWAY CARRIAGE

I forget where we found – I've a bad head for names,
It was somewhere 'twixt Rugby and Marton,
There were all sorts of fences, and very few lanes;
But I felt we were after a smart 'un.
Like a shot we passed over the Harbury road,
In the gateway I just missed a cow,
And beyond the next railing, as o'er it we strode,
I was ten paces clear of a plough.
Down that furrow with water, 'tis soundest I know,
On yon headland I'll save my horse trouble ;
I don't like the look of this fence, though it's low;
Thank goodness, we're over that double!
The ditch with a rail, near that oak-tree, was wide,
But the pace is too good to look round;
He extended himself, and took off in his stride,
And went on to the next stake and bound.
Now I fancy I see Tom catch hold of his hounds.
As we head for the wood in the hollow;
Where we know we shall find on our afternoon rounds,
Yes! they've hit off the line, and I follow
Towards the branch line from Daventry now well in sight.
Marked plainly by telegraph wire,
But the crossing is near at the gates, painted white;
Thank goodness! just what we require.
Hello ! here's a teaser, without a weak place,
And a dike on far side, brings our ride to a check,
We are down, a real purler, the quad's run his race.
And I hear myself murmur, 'I've broken my neck!'

There are gallops each season we love to think o'er,
And we price them at ten pounds a minute;
But this harmless attempt at the Image of War
Costs a penny a mile, while you're in it.

From Poems Of The Chase, *compiled by Sir Reginald Graham, 1912*

CIGARS

SIR FRANCIS HEAD (1793–1875) was a military man known as the 'Galloping Head'. Following a career culminating with the Lieutenant-Governorship of Upper Canada, he retired to a life of foxhunting in England, becoming one of the Pytchley's most notable members.

In 1861 Sir Francis published a book titled *The Horse And His Rider,* a manual of how to behave out hunting. He had firm views on health and how the hunting man should look after his body:

'A young horseman who wishes to enjoy the greatest possible amount of hunting, should ensure it by taking the greatest possible care – not of his neck, not even of his life for, as has been shown, the less he interferes with his horse in jumping the better he will go – but of his stomach.'

THE PERFECT HUNTING DIET WAS:

A big breakfast

A crust of bread for lunch

A glass of water immediately after finishing hunting

A good wholesome dinner with three or four glasses of good wine.

ALAS, TOO MANY HUNTING MEN WERE DETERMINED TO RUIN THEIR BODIES WITH THE FOLLOWING REGIME:

After breakfast, before mounting – a cigar.

On arriving at a the meet – a cigar

At two o'clock, some cold grouse, a long drain at a flask of brandy – and a cigar.

Refreshment at some road-side Inn for man and horse – a cigar

While riding home – a cigar…every hour

On reaching home: a heavy Dinner, wine…and a cigar.

Sir Francis complained, 'This constant intoxication…gradually debilitates the system of the strong man, as well as of the puny one. The first symptom of prominent decay is announced by "the nerves" which, to the astonishment of the young rider, sometimes fail so rapidly, that he is compelled to admit that "funking" has set in…'

• Sir Francis was a little peculiar on the hunting field. He caused great amusement at the Pytchley by taking his horse to covert tied to the back of a gig. This was because his groom was a heavy man and was better placed in his master's trap than on the back of his master's hunter.

NOVICE FOX-HUNTER

A memorable first day's hunting in November 1855 was enjoyed by seventeen-year-old Evelyn Wood when he joined Mr Farquharson's Hounds in Dorset.

Wood, a great soldier who was to become Field Marshal Sir Evelyn Wood VC, was back from the Crimea where he had been wounded during the siege of Sebastopol. His wound was still raw and his arm was in a sling. To make matters worse he was given a tricky 16.2 hunter to ride.

'Hounds had run fifteen minutes fast in a vale near Blandford,' Wood wrote in his autobiography. 'My horse followed them like a dog follows its master, and until a check I saw no one, and doubtless overrode the hounds.' Despite hauling on his reins with his one good hand, the horse refused to stop and charged through the middle of the pack, killing three hounds. The beast continued across a field with Wood clinging onto the saddle. Eventually it stopped.

'I rode sorrowfully back,' Wood continued. 'When I rejoined, the Master was on foot, with the Hunt servants examining casualties.'

Farquharson began to yell obscenities at the youth...until Wood was rescued by a cavalry officer who asked the Master not to be too tough on the boy since he had been severely wounded by the Russians. Bit of a war hero; you know the drill.

And that changed everything.

Farquharson dropped the dead hound he was examining. Removing his hat, he bowed to Wood and announced, 'In that case, Sir, you can ride over my hounds as many times as you like.'

Wood added that while his arm escaped injury that day in the hunting field, he managed to reopen the wound twice in the coming week: the first by tripping on the shingle at Maldon beach in Essex, and the second by falling downstairs at his barracks while in a state of inebriation.

• Kicking, or worse, killing a hound is 'the most heinous of all hunting field crimes', according to mid-twentieth century hunting writer David Brock, MFH. 'To kick the Master pales into insignificance beside it', he wrote in his 1951 book *The Young Fox-Hunter.* 'There is absolutely no excuse for kicking a hound – it is your job to prevent your horse doing so – not the hounds' job to keep out of your way. If your horse is likely to kick get rid of him without delay, no matter how good a performer he is or how fond of him you are. Just think what it means to kick and kill a hound. Perhaps he is the sole representative of a long and illustrious line of ancestors, and the Master may be counting on him to hand on his wonderful qualities to future generations. By your carelessness you kill, not one hound merely, but a huge, unborn family.'

MONKIES

IN THE EARLY NINETEENTH CENTURY there was much rivalry between the foxhunters of Warwickshire and Leicestershire. The Warwickshire Hunt considered that people who hunted at Melton Mowbray were a bunch of 'monkies' who rode as fast as they could with little regard to the technicalities of hunting. But what could the Leicestershire hunts expect without a super-hound like Trojan and a Master like John Corbet? The rivalry is revealed in the final verse of a long hunting poem by satirist Edward Goulburn (1787–1868), a lawyer and Conservative MP, who had a country seat near Stratford and hunted regularly with Corbet. Although Goulburn took a hefty swipe at Leicestershire in his ballad, his constituents must have forgiven him for he ended up as one of the counties' MPs.

> Then let Leicestershire vaunt of its far renown'd speed,
> Let them jostle or cross for a start or a lead;
> Upon selling their nags more than hunting intent,
> And scarce knowing the meaning of what is called scent.
> All declaiming at once such a shout such a yell,
> Doing only what monkies might do full as well;
> Where sport depends quite upon knowing the cover,
> And the very best run in ten minutes is over .
> May such hunting as this never fall to my lot,
> Let them race if they like it I envy them not.
> The blood of Old Trojan is all I desire,
> So give me the hounds of the Warwickshire squire!

YELLS OF ACCURSED HELL HOUNDS

THE CALPE HUNT on Gibraltar started in 1812 after the garrison chaplain the Rev. Dr Mackereth imported a couple of foxhounds – Rockwood and Ranter – to deal with the foxes that were plaguing the rock's poultry sheds. Other civilians imported more hounds, until gradually a pack was formed.

Under their first Master, Rear Admiral Elphinstone Fleeming, the Calpe gained special permission to operate in the cork forests on the Spanish mainland under British military supervision. The hunting took twice a week during between November and March, the farthest meet being about fourteen miles from Gibraltar in the Malaga Hills.

However, the Spaniards did not share the English love for hunting. A nineteenth century writer noted, 'The Spanish farmer cannot understand why so much expense is maintained, and why so much fuss of men and horses is made about an animal which he can, and indeed very often does, get rid of by a pot shot'.

The Hunt became the rock's social hub. Visitors were surprised to find so many naval officers and infantrymen who could ride. Hunting took over military life and the story is told of Governor Lieutenant-General Sir Herbert Miles who upon arriving in Gibraltar in 1913 went to garrison HQ to find none of his officers on duty. They were all hunting. He soon joined them.

Those who did not ride followed on donkey or on foot. There were picnics afterwards under the cork trees. The hunt ball was the highpoint of Gibraltar's social calendar and sometimes the Master of the Tangiers Hunt, a slightly inferior affair, was invited as a special guest.

The Calpe became the Royal Calpe in 1906 when Edward VII agreed to become patron jointly with King Alfonso XIII of Spain. Politics had little effect on the hunt. In 1937, one year into the Spanish Civil War, General Franco gave the governor, the delightfully double-barrelled Sir Charles Harington Harington, special permission for the hunt to resume. The hunt began to wane in popularity eventually fizzling out when Franco's tough border policy prevented Gibraltarians from visiting the Spanish mainland.

• The 8th Duke of Beaufort brought the Badminton pack with him when he visited Gibraltar In 1861 to recover from an illness.

• A nineteenth century travel writer called Major Edward Napier said that the Calpe Hunt was proof of the 'universal insanity of the English'. Napier's 1840 book *From Scenes and Sports In Foreign Lands* includes a letter from a Spaniard called Don Antonio Fernandez writing to a Spanish friend in London.

In a ludicrously over-the-top missive, Fernandez described a terrifying ride with the Calpe down the slopes of Andalucia's cork woods:

'Presently there was a short howl, and all the dogs began to yell and run away from the wood, as if it contained something of which they were much afraid. The horsemen immediately galloped after the dogs, I suppose to catch them, as I could see nothing else for them to pursue, whilst the latter continued to cry and run, and run and cry with all their might. My English friend had assured me that the horse I was on was a right good one, and understood his work. Alas, that I should have believed a heretic! The devil, notwithstanding all my efforts to keep him in – for why should I risk my neck in catching their dogs? – nearly pulled off my arms, and was nearly pulling me over his head, when the fortunate thought struck me of letting go the reins and seizing hold of the saddle with both hands; and to this ingenious device I attribute my preservation from utter destruction on that eventful day. Hitherto we had been galloping up a steep mountain called the Magazine Hill, and I was in hopes, by the time we got to the top, we would catch those *demonios* of dogs, and put an end to my troubles. Judge of my horror, when, on reaching the crest, I could just see their tails disappearing below the opposite declivity, which was dreadfully steep, covered with huge rocks, and broken with dry water-courses. Resigning myself to my fate, I shut my eyes and held on with redoubled energy. Methought I was going down, down to the regions of the damned with crowds of condemned spirits. Never, if I live a thousand years, shall I forget the dreadful sounds and sensations I then experienced. They tingle at this moment in every nerve. In utter darkness – for I dared not open my eyes – with the yells of those accursed hell hounds, and the screeches of the no less accursed madmen, penetrating my very brain, the clashing of the horses' hoofs over the rocks, the sudden and violent plunges of the animal I bestrode, and over which I had not the least control…I can compare the scene to nothing but the description of the defeat of Satan, by the English poet, who must have borrowed his ideas from a fox hunt.'

At the bottom of the ravine Fernandez fell off. His horse plunged into a muddy ditch and he ended up trapped beneath the animal. Other riders managed to drag him free. He was conveyed to hospital 'in a very precarious state' where he remained for several weeks. The fox went to earth in the woods.

AS PERFECT AS NATURE COULD MAKE HIM

ONE OF THE GREATEST FOXHOUNDS of them all was a stallion called Trojan, owned by eighteenth century Warwickshire Master John Corbet.

Trojan was born in 1780 and ran for nine seasons with Corbet's pack. The hunting journalist Nimrod described him as 'a hero... in chase he was as perfect as nature could make him'.

Trojan had such extraordinary strength that during a run he jumped the park wall at Chillington Hall, a superior Staffordshire stately home, 'with as much apparent ease as a greyhound crosses a hurdle'. His only vice was a tendency to chase pheasants for which he was excused because in Warwickshire 'pheasants were not much thicker than foxes'.

The 7th Earl Bathurst, writing in *The Breeding of Foxhounds* (1926), said Trojan was initially so steady, and so inclined to stay by the hunstsman's horse, that Corbet nearly got rid of him, thinking he was lazy. 'But directly he got a fox in front of him it was another matter', Bathurst wrote. 'What a wonderful dog he must have been! He could race at the head of the pack; he could hunt over dry fallows or down a road; he never tired even after the hardest day; he was never lame even from a thorn or a cut during eight seasons.'

Trojan died in 1792. He was buried under an elm tree at Corbet's Shropshire family seat Sundorne (the site is now a retail park). For years after his death Corbet and fellow members of the Hunt Club rooms in Stratford would drink a toast 'to the blood of the Trojans'.

• Trojan's ancestry is shrouded in mystery. Nimrod claims that he was sired by a hound called Trueboy owned by the 2nd Earl Spencer and bred from a bitch called Tidings purchased by Corbet at auctioneers Tattersalls. Others say that Trojan was a stray that turned up at Corbet's kennels and was so good looking he was taken out hunting. One is inclined to believe the former version.

• Not everybody admired Trojan. The hunting writer Colonel John Cook got bored with continual mentions of the dog when he went to visit Corbet's kennels. 'It was nothing but Trojan, Trojan, Trojan', Cook recalled. He did not know what the fuss was about. He added bitchily, 'I do not think Mr. Corbet's hounds would have admitted of a comparison with some of the crack packs of the present day'. Daphne Moore, author of *The Book Of The Foxhound* (J. A. Allen, 1964), the leading work on the development of the foxhound, said that judging by Trojan's portrait he was 'anything but preposessing, being sadly short of neck, curly sterned, and with far too much daylight under him.' But she added, 'Animal painters of that period were often deplorably lacking in accuracy and a knowledge of anatomy, and I like to think that Trojan was in reality a far better looking hound, his looks matching his undoubted brilliance'.

• John Corbet hunted the whole of Warwickshire at his own expense from 1791 to 1811. He was known for his sour sense of humour. When a rider allowed his horse to trample to death one of his hounds, Corbet turned to to a friend and remarked, 'Killed the best hound in my pack, that's all'. Corbet invented a system for preserving foxes in his country by paying farmer's wives for hens killed by Charlie. But Corbet was not a fearless rider. Like George III, he never jumped but waited for fences to be knocked down for him.

• Some say that the greatest hound was Brocklesby Rallywood (1843), bred in the Earl of Yarborough's Brocklesby kennels. Rallywood hunted with the Brocklesby until 1851 when he went to the Belvoir under their celebrated huntsman Will Goodall. A great great great grandson in the male line of Squire Osbaldeston's Furrier, Rallywood is regarded as the father of the modern foxhound. He hunted for nine seasons and was to become the most famous sire of the nineteenth century – he was extraordinary in that he was still siring litters at the age of ten. He was surprisingly small for his time, standing at just 23 inches. Goodall described him as 'a most beautiful little short-legged dog, exceedingly light of bone, but with beautiful legs and feet'. Rallywood died in 1852 and was buried in a flower bed in Goodall's garden. A flowering currant bush was planted on his grave.

TOUGH

As if to prove the toughness of the foxhunter, Perceval Williams, Master of the Four Burrow in Cornwall miraculously survived the First World War after receiving two bullets in his head. One was removed with a magnet but the French doctor did nothing to the other saying that it would cause no problems so long as it was left alone. Williams hunted for the rest of his life.

• Williams told a strange story of a hound called Doctor who was bitten on his tongue by an adder while cubbing: 'His tongue swelled so that he very nearly suffocated. Then the whole of the tongue dropped off, right back at the base. I had an awful job to teach him to drink; we had to hold his head under water right up to his eyes, and eventually he learned; but of course he could never drink out of a shallow dish or pond. Surprisingly, he had the most lovely voice; the same voice that he had before he lost his tongue.'

MORAL

A nineteenth century parson was scolded by his bishop for going hunting.

The parson, eager to reclaim the moral high ground, replied, 'But I gather your lordship was recently seen at a ball'.

'True,' said the bishop. 'But at a ball I am never in the same room with the dancers. '

'Like me,' said the parson. 'For I am rarely in the same field with the hounds. '

WHAT MEN DON'T LIKE

'Let the hunting lady remember that no man ever likes a woman to know as much about a horse as he thinks he knows himself.'

Anthony Trollope

DONKEYS AND CUDGELS

THE PUCKERIDGE became the subject of one of the most violent disputes in hunting history. Or as one member of the hunt described it: 'Not so much of a row, but more of a Civil War'.

By 1885 the eastern end of Puckeridge country on the Essex borders was being hunted so infrequently that the local farmers decided to start their own pack. They built kennels and found their own Master, a Mr Swindell, the unfortunately named son of a bookmaker.

The main body of the Puckeridge, headed by their Master Robert Gosling were outraged at this encroachment on their territory. They complained to the Master of Foxhounds Association, who ordered the Swindellites, as they were known, to stop hunting. A war of words followed and the Swindellites began using paramilitary techniques to harrass the opposition. Matters came to a head when the farmers drove a herd of donkeys from a travelling circus into Gosling's opening meet. The result was pandemonium.

Fights broke out between the rival hunts. By 1889 things were getting dangerous. At one meet the Swindellites laid an aniseed trail that would take Gosling's hounds over a brush fence with a hidden strand of wire on the landing side in order to bring down the horses. They planned to wait with cudgels in order to attack fallen riders. The plan misfired when hounds failed to take the bait.

Various methods were tried to resolve the dispute. The two sides even arranged an illegal prize fight between a Mr Harry Sworder for the Swindellites and Mr Frank Stacey for the Goslingites. Both trained hard but the police got wind of the contest and it was cancelled. Eventually, the MFHA found a master who was acceptable to both sides and by the turn of the century the hunts had amalgamated and the wounds had healed.

• Donkeys feature prominently at the Puckeridge. In the 1920s a Turkish donkey named Abdul used to appear at meets with children on his back. The offspring of a Turkish ammunition donkey, Abdul had been rescued as a foal following the British bombardment of Beersheba in Palestine during the First World War. The Norfolk Yeomanry had recruited him as an unofficial mascot and he spent the rest of the war on the Western Front. He was taught to wear a tin hat, to sit up like a dog and beg, and to roll over and 'die for his country'. After the war he was brought home and given to the Puckeridge Master, Major Maurice Barclay.

RED MOON

The phrase 'painting the town red' originated in Melton Mowbray in 1837 after the 3rd Marquess of Waterford and some drunken hunting chums splattered red paint on houses in the High Street. Police arrived but the Marquess escaped. He was eventually arrested and fined £100 by magistrates.

Henry Waterford (1811–59), aka the 'Mad Marquess' was the wildest hunting man in Victorian Ireland. Waterford launched a pack in Tipperary in 1849 and became famous for hunting at night. 'Whether the scent was good or bad, no day was too long for him,' explained the Irish hunting writer Bernard Fitzpatrick.

One full moon Waterford and his huntsman Johnny Ryan ran down a fox while it was jumping a high wall at twenty minutes past eleven at night. 'The music of the hounds, crossing the country at such an hour, caused no small amount of wonder,' Fitzpatrick wrote. 'A peasant who heard the Marquis's thrilling who-whoop! and the chimes of the pack, as the gallant old varmint was held high for a throw, was so terrified that he almost died of the fright; and for many a day stories were told by the country-folk about this memorable chase; and more than one amongst them firmly believed that it was his Satanic Majesty and his hell-hounds that they saw'.

Waterford sold his pack after locals with a grudge burned down his kennels. After years of drink-sodden bad behavior, his lordship married Louisa Stuart, daughter of

the 1st Baron Stuart de Rothesay. He settled down to domestic bliss at his family seat Curraghmore House and lived the remainder of his life in comparative calm.

He died aged forty-eight from a fall while hunting on high ground at Castlemorris. The Marquess's horse Mayboy stumbled at a wall, throwing him over its head. Waterford died immediately. A donkey cart was summoned, but it was nightfall before Waterford was taken off the hill. His body, stiff and cold, and still in hunting red, was draped with a dark cloak, his feet extending over the end of the cart. His faithful huntsman led the horse. To complete this epic Victorian tableau, a solitary hound walked alongside. Observers noted that there was a full moon that night. His wife admitted later that she had had a premonition of his death.

• Waterford's hunting toast was: 'Curraghmore! Sixteen and a half couples and all forrard!'

• Waterford's death caused controversy due to the fact that he had been wearing no more protection than a velvet hunting cap. From then on velvet caps remained the preserve of hunt servants and gentlemen took to wearing silk 'top' hats which were supposed to offer more protection against falls on the head, and subsequently the altogether tougher bowler hats, which became fashionable towards the end of Queen Victoria's reign. The top hat was not ideal hunting headwear. According to Colonel Richard Meysey-Thompson, author of a 1907 manual called *A Hunting Catechism*, the topper was 'an absolute nuisance in a high wind, making it impossible to keep the head erect, besides being most difficult to keep on, and most unsuitable amongst the branches and twigs of trees and hedges'.

PRUSSIANS

'I've always detested hunting because it seems to produce a particularly gross kind of caddishness in the nicest people. I don't know what it is, but they moment they dress up and get on a horse they become like a lot of Prussians.'

Lady Marchmain in Brideshead Revisited,
by Evelyn Waugh, 1945

EXTREME DEVOTION

THOMAS ASSHETON SMITH MFH, founder of the Tedworth Hunt, enjoyed his sport so much that he hunted four days a week with two packs out at the same time so he could switch from one to the other during the day.

On Assheton Smith's death aged eighty in 1858 *The Times* wrote an obituary detailing his exploits in the field; how he had been at various times master of the Quorn and the Burton and how he kept 100 couple of hounds in his kennel; and how he extended lavish hospitality to his foxhunting comrades. All this hunting had been paid for by a large private income derived from slate and copper quarries in Wales, and a 37,000 acre estate which included part of Mount Snowdon.

Assheton Smith's fixation for the noble science was too much for one *Times* reader who fired off a letter accusing the great man of wasting his life on hunting and encouraging others to do the same.

Signing himself as 'X', the correspondent snarled, 'There appears to me something artificial and unnatural, in this day, in this extreme business-like devotion to one amusement, in a gentleman getting European reputation and a kind of immortality simply and solely as a foxhunter, without the intermixture of any other element whatever is the case. Is a man who has £40,000 a year, who has all kinds of duties falling to him, doing his duty by devoting himself to the single pursuit of foxhunting?'

Assheton's Smith's muckers were outraged. Two of them, a Mr Drummond and a Mr Pritchard responded with their own letters to the newspaper. Mr D said that Mr AS had been a 'fine old English gentleman' who as well as being an unrivalled foxhunter has also been a 'capital cricketer and an excellent shot'. Morover he was 'remarkably well read' and had a 'good practical knowledge of mechanics'. Mr P added, 'Mr Smith's amusements were not confined to foxhunting, for he built and modelled some of the fastest steam yachts in England, and thus contributed in no slight degree to the shipbuilding trade of the country'.

The charge that Thomas had done nothing other than hunt wounded his widow Elizabeth terribly. She was so hurt by the *Times* letter that she commissioned a biography of her late husband to set the record straight.

It didn't really work. Assheton Smith's biographer Sir John Eardley-Wilmot (lawyer turned Member of Parliament for South Warwickshire 1874–85) evidently had the same problem as Mr X. For apart from a few passing references to Assheton Smith's yacht the book is taken up with, well, hunting…and more hunting.

On the hunting field Assheton Smith made little effort to make himself liked. He and he alone was in charge and damn anyone who dared argue with him. Despite this, everyone wanted to hunt with him. On 20 March 1840 he took his hounds down to Leicestershire for a single day with the Quorn. A record two thousand riders turned out, the biggest field ever seen in England. Eardley-Wilmot asked, 'Is it not to Mr. Assheton Smith…that foxhunting has continued, in spite of our refinement and civilisation, the powerful element in our social system?'

• The Duke of Wellington once said that Assheton Smith would have made a great cavalry officer, except that he was doing something far more important throughout the Napoleonic wars – hunting the Quorn. Napoleon met Assheton Smith in France in 1802 and introduced him as 'le premier chasseur d'Angleterre'.

• Assheton Smith's rudeness got him into trouble. While staying with the Duke of Rutland at Belvoir Castle, Assheton Smith came down to breakfast one morning before anyone else. Only one footman was on hand to serve him. This was too much for Assheton Smith who complained that the servant did not give him the attention to which he was entitled. The next morning Assheton Smith arrived at breakfast to see all the castle's footmen, in their state liveries, at stations around the table. The Duke objected to Assheton Smith rebuking his staff and was making a point. On another occasion Assheton Smith complained of the scarcity of muffins at breakfast. Next morning every footman in the castle poured into the dining room bearing a 'perpetual stream of muffins' with the unceasing chorus of, 'Muffins, Mr. Smith?'

CUBHUNTING

'CUBHUNTING gets going when enough corn is cut, generally at the beginning of September. I often think cubhunting is a bad name. Non-hunting people imagine that you are pursuing a small, rather lovable furry animal, and do not realise that the cubs have matured into fully-grown young foxes, which need an expert to tell apart from an old fox. Autumn foxhunting would be a more accurate description. Many hunting people do not understand cubhunting, and I suppose never will. It is the Master's private hunting in order to educate foxes and hounds alike, and it is also the time when the fox population is most effectively controlled.'

Former Meynell huntsman and MFH Dermot Kelly

THE CERTAIN SIGN OF A FOOL

'Not to hunt is the certain sign of a fool or an ass. Any man who is utterly
unconnected with the fox lives a little apart.'

Irish peer and writer Lord Dunsany (1878–1957)

LEAN RED SHADOWS

The cry of hounds, the holloa and the horn;
The lean red shadows where the foxes run;
To these and all their challenge we were born,
And these we leave behind us, sire to son.

This is the heritage that none can take,
The gift we hold, the gift we give again,
And this the spirit that no Time can break,
So long as England and her fields remain.

From Our Heritage, *by Will H. Ogilvie (1869–1963)*

*Lambasted by a critic as a 'turgid, pseudo-Victorian rhymester', Ogilvie was a
Scottish poet who spent much of his working life in Australia as a drover and horse
breaker. When he returned home he spent his time hunting. He was horrified by
the thought that rural Britain should ever lose its proudest tradition. A portrait of
Ogilvie posing with his fox terrier hangs in the National Library of Australia in
Canberra.*

CROSS CAT CHOPPED

THE HEADLINE 'Hounds Tore Pet Cat to Pieces' is the stuff of a Master of Foxhound's nightmares. The first time these words appeared in a British newspaper was in *The Times* in February 1967. One can only imagine that up to then nobody really cared if kitty got in the way or not; getting chopped by a pack of hounds was the sort of thing that happened to cats. But these were changing times. The antis were assembling for battle and hounds savaging pets was simply not on. Hence the headline concerning an unnamed moggy in Tiddington, Oxfordshire.

The cat's owners were a farm labourer and his wife, who bearing in mind their rural roots might have been more resilient about such a triviality. But they weren't. Mr William Cross and his other half were very cross indeed. 'The hounds ran into my back garden and set upon the cat, which was sitting on a box', Mr Cross said. 'They tore it to pieces, just like a fox.'

The hounds belonged to the South Oxfordshire Hunt. Mr John Shuter, MFH, explained that the pack had been on the scent of a fox which had just crossed the garden. He had called twice to apologise to Mr Cross, who refused to speak to him. 'I even offered to find him another cat,' Mr Shuter explained.

IRONY

'English hunters are satisfied without the death of a good fox who has shown them a first rate run. They would spare his life for another day. Englishmen are not...fond of bloody spectacles. The Spanish ladies can look on scenes in their bull fights with unblanched cheek and steady eye which would create a feeling of horror and disgust in the heart of an Englishman. The dark ages have passed away from us and we read with loathing the accounts of cruelties practiced by even kings and queens in less civilised times However, the ardour, the excitement, the uncertainty in the fox chase, its difficulties, its labours, its enlivening influence upon the mind, its tendencies to promote good fellowship and good feeling amongst all classes, claim for this sport above all others the distinguishing title of The Noble Science'.

Baily's Magazine of Sports and Pastimes, *1861*

A PECULIAR AFFAIR

'THE NAMING OF HOUNDS is a peculiar affair. It is impossible to generalise as to the names accepted as suitable. Peter Beckford, in 1781, wrote *Thoughts On Hunting*, and in it he gave a list of hounds' names. This list is accepted as one that can be used. Adjectives are found such as Able, Anxious; nouns such as Bowler, Rival; professions such as Magistrate, Woodman. Christian names appeared later, such as Samuel and Alfred, but in no great profusion. There have been Masters of Hounds with a classical tendency who have borrowed from mythology, Charon, Hercules; and others who have added obscure names such as Sassifras, Rataplan. Birds and plants are sometimes represented, Widgeon and Saxifrage. In fact, there is a wide choice, but on the other hand, an overall inexplicable feeling as to what is acceptable. The usual practice is to give a hound the initial letter of its sire or dam. If possible the first two letters of the hound's name are the initial letters of both sire and dam. All the litter, say, of Topper out of Resolute could be named Tracer, Tragic, Trier and so on. This helps memorise the pedigree and so also does a method, following an idea suggested by the name of a parent, e.g. the produce of the litter out of a bitch called Widgeon would well be called Wildfowl, Water-rail, Whinchat, etc. Two-syllable words are preferred because they are easier to call out. Often one hears surprise expressed as to the huntsman knowing all the hounds apart, but really there is little difficulty as they are nearly always marked in colour differently, except, of course, in some packs where all the hounds are white. In that case the make and shape offer clues.'

Lord Knutsford, In Praise of Hunting, *Hollis & Carter, 1960.*

Thurstan Holland-Hibbert, 4th Viscount Knutsford (1888–1976), a barrister, was in turn Master of the Trinity Food Beagles, the Terne Valley Foxhounds, the Avon Vale Foxhounds, and the V. W. H. He judged hounds at Peterborough.

• Hunting authors have a habit of presenting endless lists of hounds names at the conclusion of their books. The Edwardian writer C. F. P. McNeill, MFH, included no less than 5,000 names in *The Unwritten Laws Of Foxhunting*. The stranger ones included: Alien, Anodyne, Bajazet, Cactus, Catspaw (the indignity of it!), Chastity, Chuckaway, Cocktail, Crockery, Cynical, Dabchick, Diary, Dicebox, Duplex, Endive, Epigraph, Etiquette, Eyebrow, Eyelash, Faggott (not sure you'd get away with that these days), Fleshy, Foljamb, Footstool, Freakish, Gymnast, Handcuff, Hyphen, Keynote, Makeshift, Mendicant, Moisten, Paragraph, Paraphrase, Quidnunc, Rateable, Rhinewine, Sandwich, Sealskin, Tabloid, Toothsome, Warpaint, Whitewash, and Yashmak (very suitable in these diverse times.)

HAPPY

'Happy are they who go out hunting to please themselves,
not to astonish others.'

*The fictitious MFH Mr. Facey Romford quoted in Robert
Surtees' 1865 novel* Mr Romford's Hounds

COW CHASING

The claim that cows enjoy following hounds featured in an entertaining exchange at Brighton County Court in 1953.

During a hunt trespass case, Mr Fred Cockerill, Huntsman of the Southdown, claimed that it was common for cows to stop grazing and follow hounds as a pack chased a fox across their pasture.

Judge Harold Brown: 'What's the attraction? Cows must be very slow animals'.

Mr Cockerill: (Trying hard) 'I don't know. But I have seen cows go behind hounds and follow them into the next field.'

Southdown joint master Ian Askew was being sued for damages by farmers Tom Wood and Richard Horner who had to pacify sixteen cows after the hunt crossed their land. In his summing up Judge Brown took the hunt's side and said that Askew was 'completely free from all moral blame'. But unfortunately, the farmers had prohibited the hunt after two previous incidents and, although Mr Askew said he had taken this to apply to horses and followers and not to hounds, he was strictly liable and ordered to pay a token £10 damages.

FOWL PLAY

RURAL MYTH: Legend has it a fox can hypnotise a roosting hen so that it becomes so giddy that it will fall out of a tree. The fox is said to take his brush in his mouth and run circles beneath the fowl so that the mesmorised creature eventually tumbles from its perch.

RURAL MYTH 2: A fox will get rid of fleas by gathering a mouthful of sheep's wool from hedges. It will then submerge itself up to its nose in a pond until the fleas have migrated from his body up to the wool. He then lets go of the wool and emerges flea-free from the water.

NEVER DOGS

DOGS ARE CONSIDERED UNCLEAN IN ISLAM. If a Moslem is licked by a dog then the Koran advises that the person must wash themselves seven times and rub themselves with earth before they are properly clean. Which leads on to the story of an English traveller in Arabia, who was being entertained by a sheikh. They were eating gazelle that had been coursed by the sheikh's saluki pack. The traveller enquired how his host could justify eating meat that had been killed by a dirty dog. The sheikh replied gravely, 'A saluki is not a dog; he is a hound. And hounds are *never* dirty'.

DON'T DARE DIE

THE REV. J. P. SEABROOKE, vicar of Waltham, in the thick of Leicestershire hunting country, towards the end of the nineteenth century, promised his parishioners when he accepted the living that he would hunt only two days a week. Once ensconced, with no noticeable effect to his conscience, he cunningly altered this to four half days a week with the Belvoir on his grey called Top-Bar. It didn't matter because his parishioners all hunted as well. It was said that during Seabrooke's long tenure nobody would dare get married or be buried on a hunting day.

KILLER PACK

You did not want to mess with the hounds of Colonel Giles Eyre, who kept a private pack in Galway in the early 1800s. In common with the Irish squires of his day, Eyre was a bit of a nutter. He spent a fortune trying to breed the strongest and fiercest hounds in Ireland. His favoured cross was bloodhound with mastiff. He created some terrifying beasts. A contemporary writer pointed out, 'The pack's courage and temper became so high that they would hardly brook correction'. Eyre's experiment ended in tragedy. One night his elderly huntsman Nick Carolan, thoroughly sloshed from too much poteen, tottered into the kennel to say goodnight to his hounds and passed out in the straw. Next morning there was barely a trace of old Nick. The pack had eaten him, boots an' all.

• The ghost of a huntsman called Dick Down, who was eaten by hounds in the eighteenth century, inhabited the coverts around the park at the Devonshire estate of Hayne, near Dartmoor.

• An early nineteenth century huntsman called Holmes, from Essex, was eaten by hounds after he went into the kennel one night to break up a fight. All that remained was his bones, boots and whip.

WARE WIRE

Foxhunting changed for ever with the introduction of wire fencing in the second half of the nineteenth century. First, plain wire arrived at the end of the 1850s. And in 1862 the dreaded barbed wire made its debut.

Riders now had to look carefully where they were going. No longer could 200 horsemen, as in the glory days of the Billesdon Coplow Run, charge with hounds for more than twenty miles in a straight line without stopping; no longer could huge, tired hunters, unwilling to jump, be forced through thick hedges. For now jumps had to be examined for wire and gates had to be opened.

In 1862, a group of landowners in Leicester and Northamptonshire circulated a leaflet to farmers: 'We, the undersigned…have observed with deep regret the increasing practice of fencing with wire as a substitute for rails, as well as for stopping gaps. This kind of fencing is so dangerous, both to horses and their riders, that if the custom becomes general it will entirely put an end to fox-hunting.' The protest had little effect and the wire remained.

In Parliament, foxhunting politician Lord Henry Bentinck railed, 'The curse to hunting in the present day is wire, in many cases put up without necessity or without regard to common sense'.

The British Farmer's Magazine of 1863 deplored the way wire had created ill-feeling between 'the two important classes' of landlord and tenant.

'However effectual wire may prove in stopping the career of a bullock, it is a yet more decided impediment to the passage of a horse; or, in other words, no man can cross a country where this kind of fencing is suffered to remain up during the winter or hunting months.'

But the magazine had sharp words for foxhunters. 'The nobility and gentry who hunt in the shires have a simple remedy for the evil in their own hands. Let them not be afraid of putting those hands in their pockets. The village blacksmith would take up the wires and put them down again, at a cost that would not be ruinous. If foxhunters are too selfish to pay for their own amusement, they deserve to lose it.'

The hunting historian Roger Longrigg sights three reasons why wire gained popularity in hunting country:

1. Small tenant farmers could afford no other kind of fencing.
2. Socially resentful farmers strung it up purely to be bloody-minded and screw up hunting.
3. Cynical this, but possibly true: landowners, pretending to be friends of foxhunting in order to retain local popularity, allowed wire to be used so that they could save money to spend on their hunting establishments in other countries.

In the early days of wire Masters tried to persuade farmers to build fences or plant hedges instead. Some Masters like Lord Dudley in Worcestershire replaced wire with rails until his back was turned and all his tenants returned to wire. Unsurprisingly, there was little wire where hunts were chiefly populated by farmers. Likewise wire was rare where a Master was extremely popular, as in Warwickshire during Lord Willoughby de Broke's reign.

Some hunts had wire committees who negotiated with farmers to remove wire during the hunting season and put it back up in the spring when livestock was turned out. Wire committees were also responsible for marking wired fences. But committees could become lax. This was dangerous for visitors who might jump an unmarked wired fence.

'All wire should be marked or none at all,' said Charles Richardson, hunting editor of *The Field*. 'It is better to have no danger signals than a short supply.' Writing in 1908, Richardson admitted that wire was a 'recognised evil' that was here to stay. 'Barbed wire is now such a necessity...that it is no use attempting to ignore its existence.'

• Barbed wire properly entered the world in America in 1875 when a pushy young Illinois salesman called John W. Gates set off for Texas with a supply of his latest product. Although the invention was a couple of years old, no one had yet tried to sell it seriously. The hard-bitten Texan ranchers took one look at Gates's wire and laughed him off. How could a few strands of wire hold in their feisty longhorns? Gates ignored their jibes. Using barbed wire, he turned the town square of San Antonio into a huge corral. He filled it with the most bad-tempered cattle he could find, and challenged the ranchers to stampede them through the wire. Despite much shooting and hollering, the beasts stubbornly refused to budge. It was a wild publicity stunt that paid off. The cow's ability to learn fast made Gates a millionaire and changed the face of the world's countryside for ever.

A MOST REASONABLE BEAST

The oldest English book on hunting is *The Master of Game* written in 1406 by Edward of Norwich, 2nd Duke of York, grandson of Edward III. Much of the book is plagiarised from the French medieval hunting classic *Livre de Chasse* of Gaston Phoebus.

Edward added five dog-mad chapters of his own, including this homily to hounds: 'A hound is a most reasonable beast, and best knowing of any beast that ever God made... A hound is of great understanding and of great knowledge, a hound hath great strength and great goodness, a hound is a wise beast and a kind one. A hound has a great memory and great smelling, a hound has great diligence and great might, a hound is of great worthiness and of great subtlety, a hound is of great lightness and of great perseverance , a hound is of good obedience, for he will learn as a man all that a man will teach him. A hound is full of good sport ; hounds are so good that there is scarcely a man that would not have of them...'

• The next treatise on English foxhunting appeared in 1674 titled The *Gentleman's Recreation* by Nicholas Cox, who strongly believed that hunting was good for you: 'No music can be more ravishingly delightful than a pack of hounds in full cry'. The pursuit of the fox was a healthy rural pastime compared to the 'besotting sensualities and wicked debaucheries of a city...where there is little other recreation but what women, wine and a bawdy play can afford them...' But Cox warned that too much hunting could do your head in. 'There is great danger, lest we be transported with this pastime, and so ourselves grow wild, haunting the woods, till we resemble the beasts which are citizens of them.' A gentleman should have other hobbies besides hunting. 'Continual conversation with dogs' was not good for a man.

MEMORABLE DAY

An entertaining run was had by the York and Ainsty Hunt on 10 February 1921, when a fox fled through the gardens of Copgrove Hall, Harrogate, seat of Admiral Sir Francis Bridgeman, and crashed through a pane of glass into the admiral's greenhouse. Much to the admiral's horror, the fox was followed by the entire pack. None of the hounds was injured but the greenhouse was a terrible mess. The fox escaped.

FAST EMPRESS

People were so keen to see royalty hunting during Victorian times that when Elizabeth, Empress of Austria, visited the Pytchley in 1878 a field of 500 was watched by 15,000 followers. The anorexic Empress carried a black fan and much to the horror of English women, she drank beer and smoked cheroots. Before joining the Pytchley it took her maid an hour to sew her into a chamois body stocking. The Empress adored hunting. 'I do not mind the falls,' she said, 'But I will not scratch my face'.

A MAGNIFICANT DAY

LORD MIDDLETON'S HOUNDS enjoyed a magnificent run in December 1861 when they chased a fox for nearly forty miles across East Yorkshire. No less than three railways were crossed and three river swum.

The hunt met at Middleton's seat Birdsall Hall, near Malton. Hounds drew in Lang Hill Wood and set off to Grimston, across the Driffield Railway, then on to Norton, back to Menethorpe, across the Scarborough Railway, and on to the River Derwent in the North Riding.

The field now lost the pack. After crossing the Derwent, hounds continued to Castle Howard, into the Vale of Pickering where the field regained sight of them. Then it was over the Thirsk Railway and the River Rye. By the time night fell, hounds had crossed the Costa Beck and were still going strong.

At this point the field gave up and went home to bed.

Later that night, a long way up on the moors above the village of Pickering, local people were astonished to witness a fox hunt in the dark. How it ended is uncertain for no sign of the fox was ever found. Hunt staff took all of next day rounding up the exhausted hounds.

ANOTHER RURAL MYTH?

Country folk say that a fox has sometimes been known to hide in the carcase of a recently killed sheep.

THE KEEN FOXHUNTER'S MISCELLANY

POOR MAD HARRY

The 4th Marquess of Hastings, Master of the Quorn 1866–8, was a tragic-comic character of nineteenth century hunting. 'Mad Harry', as friends knew him, was a legend in his own lunchtime. He was described as 'very extragavant, very weak and usually very drunk indeed'. He is said to have breakfasted on mackerel bones soused in gin. Out hunting, Hastings was renowned for being late, frequently arriving with hounds at 1 pm, the rest of the field having been waiting in from eleven. Once Hastings was asked to blow his horn: 'Impossible – do you want to see me sick in sight of the whole field?' The Quorn's members got fed up with him but since he paid for everything nobody could bring themselves to make an official complaint.

Harry Hastings' love life was nicely dysfunctional. In 1864 he caused a scandal by marrying a girl called Lady Florence Paget, who was already engaged to another man, a Lincolnshire landowner called Harry Chaplin.

Lady Florence and her fiancé had gone shopping at the fashionable London department store Marshall and Snelgrove. While Mr Chaplin waited for his bride-to-be at one entrance, Florence exited by a back door where Lord Hastings' brougham was waiting for her. The carriage took her to St George's Church, Hanover Square, where she and Hastings were married. Hastings took her back to his family seat Donington Hall, a hideous barracks in Leicestershire. There he introduced her to a lifestyle of cock-fighting, racing, hunting and stupendous parties during which the Marquess's jockeys would climb onto the dining room table and dance the hornpipe.

Harry's thirst for alcohol eventually did him in. Having lost most of his fortune gambling, he died of a collapsed liver in 1868 whilst still in tenure of the Quorn. He was aged only twenty-six.

> • Harry Chaplin, the poor sod left in the lurch at Marshall and Snelgrove, was a parson's son who inherited a Lincolnshire estate from his bachelor uncle. Chaplin was at Oxford with the Prince of Wales and became a leading member of the prince's racing, hunting and gambling set. He was a large man and weighed seventeen stone in later years. Life as a country squire was not enough for him and he became an MP. At the age of seventy-six he received a peerage. Chaplin voiced the feelings of the hunting fraternity when he declared that 'the only wire in a hunting country should be on champagne bottles, and this should be ready to come off at a moment's notice'. Chaplin is also the man who uttered the often quoted lines, 'It is easier to find a good Prime Minister than a good huntsman, and heaven knows that either is difficult enough'.

YELLOW

BOXING ARISTOCRAT LORD LONSDALE was a great hunting man. Master of the Quorn 1893–98, he was known as the Yellow Earl because of his penchant for the colour. He laid on a fleet of yellow carriages to convey his house parties to meets and, just in case, a yellow ambulance. His staff wore canary yellow livery with dark blue facings and white buckskin breeches and white beaver top hats. Lonsdale was an MFH with attitude and an autocratic style that was not appreciated by all. He complained of too many women out hunting and 'impudent farmers' who requested 'a greater share in the running of the hunt'.

One day a Quorn farmer caught Lonsdale as he was cutting some barbed wire on a fence.

'Taking down my wire is not hunting, my Lord,' the farmer said.

'No, but it is half way to it, so come and give me a hand there's a good fellow'. The farmer was so taken aback by Lonsdale's charm that he helped the peer to remove the wire.

Lord Lonsdale lived off more than £100,000 a year earned from coal mines on his estates. He breakfasted on a glass of brandy and half a bottle of vin blanc; his annual cigar bill was in the region of £3,000. He issued the Quorn's followers with new hunt buttons bearing the letter Q topped with the Lonsdale coronet. Some subscribers refused to wear them. But not all was bad about Lonsdale. He was the man who saved the Cottesmore in 1915 when he arrived as Master with an injection of much-needed cash. He retired in 1921 aged sixty-three and never hunted again. Lord Lonsdale's hunting toast was: 'To the Ladies and Foxhunting'.

AND WHAT'S WRONG WITH THAT?

Landowner baronet Sir William Eden, father of Prime Minister Anthony, who led the South Durham Hounds for nine seasons during the late nineteenth century, resigned his mastership because he could stand no longer the oafish and testosteronic qualities of the subscribers. Sir William was a delicate man, semi-professional watercolourist and art collector with excellent taste. He collected works by Renoir and Degas. He deplored Hooray Henry behaviour. After his resignation he wrote of the South Durham: 'Whisky and water, horses and cigars, and occasionally a pretty woman…that was their taste, the sum total of their education'.

WHOLESOME EXERCISE

The first subscription pack in America was the Gloucester Foxhunting Club, founded in 1766 in Gloucester County, New Jersey, across the river from Philadelphia.

The club's first meet attracted twenty-seven riders. The initial idea seems to have been an opportunity for country farmers to entertain the town's businessmen.

Philadelphia's business elite hurried to join. They each paid five pounds per year for the upkeep of the pack. When a fox was killed, the members passed round a hat for the huntsman.

In 1769 a negro called Natt became whipper-in. The club paid him £50 per annum, and gave him a house and a horse. They also agreed to insure him in case of accidents.

For a while, the Gloucester was a simple affair, but it didn't take long for the club to start emulating its English counterparts. In 1774 members adopted a uniform of dark brown coat with 'lapelled dragoon pockets, white buttons and frock sleeves, buff waistcoat and breeches, and a black velvet cap'. They hunted with sixteen couple of hounds.

Although temporarily interrupted by the War of Independence, during which twenty-two members helped to form the First Troop of the Philadelphia City Cavalry, the club continued to hunt into the

nineteenth century. But by 1800 the emphasis was as much on having a good party as a good hunt. The hunt historian reported that only half the forty members regularly followed hounds. The other half would turn up only for the dinners which were 'cheerful and exhilarating festive occasions' noted for their 'sparkling goblets of Madeira'. The club disbanded around 1820.

• The first man to import hounds into America was Robert Brooke, an English parson from Southampton , who introduced his pack in 1650. Brooke became governor of Maryland. Around this time, European red foxes were brought into America for the specific purpose of hunting. The first organised hunt in America was started by ex-pat aristocrat Thomas, 6th Baron Fairfax in 1747. Fairfax owned extensive estates in Virginia. Presidents Thomas Jefferson and George Washington both hunted hounds. Washington went out three times a week until civic duties took over his life. Today there are 177 hunts in thirty-five states, including the Red Rock Hounds (founded 1980) who operate in the most unlikely hunting country in the high desert outside Reno, Nevada. There are 20,000 registered members of hunts across America with the number rising rapidly every year. The greatest threat to American foxhunting comes not from 'antis' but from urbanisation which takes large chunks of country every year.

• The oldest subscription pack in north America is the Montreal Hunt, founded in 1826, and now known as Le Club de Chasse à Courre de Montréal owing to its largely French membership.

• The oldest surviving subscription pack in the United States is the Rose Tree Foxhunting Club, founded in 1859 at the Rose Tree Inn, in Delaware County, Pennsylvania. It is still a thriving fox hunt.

GREATS

The twelve greatest foxhounds of all time, according to early twentieth century dog writer Robert Leighton:

Mr Corbet's Trojan (1780), Lord Middleton's Vanguard (1815), Mr Osbaldeston's Furrier (1820), Lord Henry Bentinck's Contest (1848), Lord FitzHardinge's Cromwell (1855), Mr Drake's Duster (1844), Sir Richard Sutton's Dryden (1849), the Duke of Rutland's Senator (1862), the Duke of Rutland's Weathergauge (1874), the Earl of Coventry's Rambler (1874), Mr E. P. Rawnsley's Freeman (1884), the Grafton Woodman (1892).

MUSIC

A STORY IS TOLD OF A LONDONER who watched a hunt while on a day trip to the countryside. A hunt follower stands beside him and, referring to the baying of the pack, says, 'What glorious music! Don't you hear it?'

'Music?' replies the Londoner. 'I can't hear no music for the yelping of those confounded dogs.'

OBSESSIVE

ENGLAND'S MOST OBSESSIVE hunt follower was Jem Hastings, a nineteenth century tailor from Cheltenham who covered miles following hounds. Hastings was so quick that he was nearly always in at the kill. Running was his antidote to sitting cross-legged for hours on end stitching clothes. According to a contemporary account, Hastings 'knew every bank dingle bush and briar, watched with unabated zeal his cubs, as he always called them, and could tell to a certainty how many brace of foxes were killed each season, dogs and vixens. He was a perfect living chronicle of all the great runs and all other hunting matters'.

During the week Hastings followed Lord Segrave's Gloucestershire pack, and on Saturdays he went to the Duke of Beaufort's. Lord Segrave was so impressed by Hastings' energy that he offered him work as an earth-stopper. He turned the job down because he said he needed his nights to do his tailoring.

• Hastings had a mischievous streak. He once put an aniseed drag on the back of one of the London coaches in order to give his dog some exercise. His dog was joined by a dozen more with the result that the horses bolted and the coach turned over.

CHARLIE

THE FOX earned its soubriquet 'Charlie' after Charles James Fox, late eighteenth century English Prime Minister. Fox himself never hunted, but his friends found it all the more amusing that a hunted animal should be named after a non-hunting man. Fox hated the countryside. He was a committed townie and away from politics his main hobbies were gambling and prostitutes, preferably French.

Most of Fox's friends in the Whig party loved hunting. The first Earl Spencer, a great Whig, founded the Pytchley (1750) and Earl Fitzwilliam, heir to the Marquis of Rockingham, founded the The Fitzwilliam, or Milton, (1769).

• Medieval poet Geoffrey Chaucer called the fox Dan Russell, or Master Russet, after his reddish colour.

A VERY GOOD DEATH

'I say to parents, especially to wealthy parents, "Don't give your son money. As far as you can afford it, give him horses". No one ever came to grief – except honourable grief – through riding horses. No hour of life is lost that is spent in the saddle. Young men have often been ruined through owning horses, or through backing horses, but never through riding them: unless, of course, they break their necks, which, taken at a gallop, is a very good death to die.'

From My Early Life, by *Winston Churchill, 1930*

• Churchill told a good story about the Regimental Riding Master at Aldershot, a 'terrible tyrant' named nicknamed Jocko. One of Churchill's colleagues, a senior subaltern, had inserted in the *Aldershot Times* an advertisement which read: 'Major, Professor of Equitation, East Cavalry Barracks. Hunting taught in twelve lessons and steeple-chasing in eighteen'. Jocko did not see the joke. Churchill commented, 'This had drawn upon him a flood of ridicule which perhaps led him to suppose that every smile that ever flitted across the face of one of his riding-school class was due to some inward satisfaction at his expense'.

OLD COBS

'IN MY YOUNGER DAYS IN HUNTING, it was always drilled into me that your hounds when running should be able to be covered by a tablecloth.'

'It doesn't matter which hunting horn you blow, you can only get one musical note out of them: F or A. Ted Hill at the Barlow could put two horns to his lips and blow both together, and it was the most marvellous sound ever heard in your life…he used a Cotswold and Goodall, as one had an F note, and the other had an A note.'

'As huntsmen, we do live well. It's the same as being a jockey: if you can keep off the whisky and the women – you do need plenty of them, but not too much – then we do live well. As a huntsman you're out in the open doing something that you love. Some go over the top with whisky and women. I learnt something very early in married life: if you keep a thoroughbred in your stable you don't go buggering about riding old cobs.'

Nuggets of wisdom from Tom Normington, Huntsman of the Grafton Foxhounds, 1972–1995

A DELICATE SHADE OF COBALT

Quoth I to my hunter, good steed, have a care!
The season's first meet is today.
My boots are all shiny, my red coat is new,
And my personal pride is completed in you;
Now correct be thy manners, I pray.
But he squealed and he bucked, and right over his head
All into the mire like a rocket I sped.

Quoth I to my hunter, good steed, have a care!
When to covert so slowly we jog.
The pack will press round thee, but heed my appeals!
Restrain thy resentment, nor suffer they heels
To endanger the life of a dog.
In vain my advice. Right in front of the Master
The pick of the pack at his heels met disaster.

Quoth I to my hunter, good steed, have a care!
This brook is deep, muddy and broad.
Thy pace should be fast and thy spring should be high,
And we'll cut them all down if across it we fly,
While the rest are in search of a ford.
Yes! The water was deep – there was mud there galore,
As I found to my cost when I scrambled ashore.

Quoth I to my hunter, good steed, have a care!
The hounds I can see are at fault.
Now slacken thy pace, or the Master, I fear,
Will not cease from rebuke till the whole atmosphere
Turns a delicate shade of cobalt.
But his mouth was as iron, and his neck like a bull,
As he charged right amont them – and my cup was full.

Quoth I to my hunter, good steed, have a care!
Or my crop I shall use with a will.
Though smooth be thy paces and shapely they form,
They only are handsome that handsome perform,
And thou has done everything ill.
But I felt for such faults he could ne'er make amend,
So got rid of the brute for ten pounds to a friend.

The New Hunter, *by Francis Monckton*

Lieutenant Monckton, of the Scots Guards, hunted with the Albrighton.
He was killed in action at Ypres in 1914 aged twenty-four.

ODDS AGAINST DEATH

Hunting journalist William Scarth Dixon, writing in his
1900 memoir *The Sport Of Kings*, claimed
to have calculated the odds against
having a serious fall out hunting:

A man who goes out hunting having a fall at all: 10 – 1 against

Either he or his horse being hurt: 80 – 1

The rider being hurt: 480 – 1

The rider suffering a broken bone: 15,760 – 1

A fatal accident: Anything between 115,200 – 1 to 480,000-1

How Dixon worked this out is unknown.

HUNTING SCENE

O NE OF THE MOST POPULAR DESIGNS offered by the great Edwardian tattoo artist Sutherland Macdonald was an English hunting scene with numerous horses and red-coated riders pursuing a fox. He could make it as big as you liked and used it to cover the backs of various young cavalrymen. Sutherland learned his trade in the British Army. He had a surprisingly posh clientele and worked out of a studio in Jermyn Street in London's West End until his death in 1937.

WHAT THE PRESS SAID BEFORE THE BAN...

'THE SHAMEFUL STATE OF OUR PUBLIC SERVICES, defence, crime, Iraq...all must vie for attention with the question of whether a tiny minority should be allowed to dress up in red coats and gallop in pursuit of small bundles of russet fur...we find hunting both distasteful and somewhat absurd. But we also believe passionately in the principle of live-and-let-live and are appalled at the way the concerns of the countryside are ignored by an uncomprehending political elite. We also believe the hatred Labour MPs have for hunting owes more to class-war prejudice than any rational concern for the fate of the fox'. Daily Mail *editorial, 16 September 2004, the day after the pro-hunting demo in Parliament Square.*

'The Commons has spoken, not once but seven times. The Lords may stage a rearguard action but with little hope and less legitimacy. Diana is vanquished. Nimrod is slain...a hunting ban reveals the inability of a mature democracy to tolerate disagreement without recourse to compulsion'. *Simon Jenkins*, The Times, *2004.*

'There are a thousand and one big issues worrying *Sun* readers. Foxhunting is not one of them. So why is Parliament wasting so much time debating the subject?' Sun *editorial, July 1, 2003.*

...WHAT THE PRESS SAID AFTER THE BAN

'TONY BLAIR, EVER ANXIOUS TO PLEASE EVERYBODY, allowed a law to be pushed through that gave the bully boys of the left the pleasing impression that they had handed out a bloody nose to the middle classes. Mr Blair himself didn't give a fig one way or the other...'. *Sunday Express, February 2005.*

'Judging from Saturday, the effect of the hunting ban is that tens of thousands of people are going to charge around the countryside saying that they are NOT hunting. And thousands are going to charge after them saying that they ARE. In all the confusion it is worth remembering... the original reason for all this... was to stop being cruel to foxes... Human beings are always clever enough to alter their behaviour when faced with a stupid rule, thereby defeating its purpose...' *William Hague*, News of the World, *February 2005.*

'Hunters and their opponents have long done us great service with their emblematic confrontations defusing deeper rifts: toffs versus oiks, country v town, Whigs v Tories, EastEnders v Emmerdale....We admit to delight that the law is clearly unenforceable and that hunting has so far proceeded undisturbed. If parliament intended to protect animals, it fell at the first fence.' The Observer, *February 2005.*

• In April 2009, the *Guardian,* the Labour Party's favourite newspaper, carried a poll in which 72% of readers said that the Hunting Act should be repealed.

BROKE

THE AGRICULTURAL DEPRESSION of the early 1880s, coupled with outbreaks of foot and mouth, brought hard times to England's hunting community. Crop prices and rents went down and landowners struggled to pay for their hunting. Things were so bad in the Warwickshire Hunt that a baronet called Sir Charles Mordaunt was inspired to write a poem titled *The Lament Of The Squires:*

> Broke! broke, broke,
> Are the lords of the soil and the squires;
> And alas! that my tongue should utter,
> The thoughts that arise in the Shires.
>
> O, bad for the nobleman's son,
> When his stud is to Tattersall's sent!
> O, bad for the squire, too,
> When his tenants can pay him no rent!
>
> And the eager crowds go on
> To Ascot and Newmarket still;
> But Oh! for the touch of the vanished coin,
> And the sound of the gold in the till.
>
> Broke! broke, broke,
> Are the lords of this cold, clay land;
> And slender's the chance that the money lost
> Will ever come back to hand.

• Sir Charles Mordaunt was a Warwickshire Member of Parliament with a fiery temper. In his early thirties he married Harriet Moncrieffe, twenty-two-year-old daughter of a Scottish baronet. Pretty Harriet attracted the attention of that old dog the Prince of Wales, the future Edward VII. One summer's day in 1868, Sir Charles returned home to his mansion Walton Hall to find the young Prince watching Lady M as she demonstrated her carriage-driving skills. Sir Charles ordered the Prince to leave, dragged his wife onto the lawn and had her ponies shot in front of her. This he thought would cure her inattentiveness. Wrong. Lady M turned out to be a right slapper and admitted to sleeping with several men, including the POW. While her husband had been out foxhunting she had had been shagging everything in sight. Harriet's parents declared she must be mad and locked her away in a lunatic asylum. Sir Charles sued for divorce citing the prince, who claimed that Harriet and he were no more than friends and escaped cross-examination in court because of who he was. Sir Charles was refused a divorce on account of his wife's insanity. In a subsequent action, Sir Charles got his divorce when one of his wife's lovers, Viscount Cole (bribed by the prince), admitted adultery. Harriet spent the rest of her life in the bin and Sir Charles got remarried to the sixteen-year-old virgin daughter of a parson. An every day story of hunting folk…

NERVOUS MOMENT

THE BLACKMORE VALE HOUNDS narrowly avoided ending up a nasty mess in December 1884 after they cornered a fox on a railway track in the mouth of a tunnel. Just as the pack settled into their kill, the 12.48 from Gillingham chose the moment to make its appearance. To make things even more inconvenient, the drama happened in the middle of a snowstorm.

Thankfully the train driver managed to spot the hounds in time. 'It was a narrow escape', wrote one of the masters in the Blackmore Vale's journal. 'The driver applied his powerful vacuum brake, and (no doubt much to the surprise of his passengers) was able to stop the engine…the hounds crossed before and behind the train, utterly regardless of their danger. Not one was injured ; but it was a most nervous moment for the field, who watched it all from the bridge.'

Otherwise, it was a mercifully dull day. The journal concluded, 'The day was bitterly cold, and there was no sport in the afternoon.'

REMARKABLE ENMITY TOWARDS FOXES

The lampooning of foxhunters began in 1711 when the *Spectator* created a character called Sir Roger de Coverley, a Tory squire, famed for 'his remarkable enmity towards foxes'. One of de Coverley's tricks was to rob foxes from neighbouring countries, bag 'em up and then release them into his own country.

PLEBEIAN ANCESTRY

'A WHIPPER-IN'S TASK is not one requiring great technical skill. What it does require is a quick brain, an eye for a country, a great deal of common sense, a keen sense of discipline and, perhaps above all, a sense of humour. There is little real enjoyment on a cold December night – especially if you are already wet to the skin, tired, hungry, riding a leg-weary horse of extremely plebeian ancestry, and twelve miles from kennels – to be had out of being sent three miles in the wrong direction to search a hilly forest of some thousand acres for a foxhound, which you, personally, think is an encumbrance to the pack. If, on your eventual arrival at the kennels four hours later, you can laugh on being told that "Lawful was in by half past three", then you are well on the road to being a whipper-in.'

D. W. E. Brock MFH, from To Hunt The Fox. *David Brock was an outspoken twentieth century hunting writer. At various times he was Master of the East Sussex and the Thurles and Kilshane in Tipperary, Ireland.*

• Brock held strong views on point-to-points. 'The hunt concerned should view the point-to-point meeting not as a source of income but merely as a means of entertaining the farmers, and perhaps also the stoppers and keepers: all profits should go to this cause, where they will eventually do far more good than they would were they allotted to general hunt funds, no matter how sorely in need of them the latter may be. A large credit balance at the bank is useless for foxhunting if there is no land to hunt over, while the enthusiastic goodwill of the farmers will make up for any overdraft'. Many point to point riders had little interest in hunting and used racing as a vehicle for bringing them fame. 'They bring with them into the hunting field a spirit of competition which is alien to it and a regard for the horse which leaves no room for a regard for the hounds, the more important cog in the fox-hunting machine.'

• Brock also came up with the line: 'If your groom lives in a pig-sty so will your horse'.

NONSENSE

OTIS FERRY IS ONE OF THE MOST CONTROVERSIAL FIGURES in English hunting. The son of rock star Brian Ferry, Otis arouses strong emotions. Some consider him a political revolutionary; others say he is a public school trouble maker. But whatever the case, those who hunt with young Ferry in the South Shropshire say that he is one of the finest huntsmen of his generation who will give you the best sport that the law allows.

Marlborough-educated Ferry came to prominence in the early days of New Labour as whipper-in with the Middleton. He was arrested in 2002 for demonstrating at the constituency home of Prime Minister Tony Blair in Sedgefield, County Durham.

Two years later Otis and seven other pro-hunting protesters achieved international fame by illegally entering the House of Commons chamber while the anti-hunting bill was in the final stages of debate. They infiltrated the Parliament buildings by posing as construction workers. Otis was arrested and convicted of public order offences. He was fined £350 and given an eighteen-month conditional discharge. Many people found Otis and chums' antics delightfully amusing. All except for the silly *Guardian* who made the ridiculously over the top comment that their actions were little different to those of Goering's pilots who had launched aerial bombing raids on Westminster during the war.

In 2008, in what was to turn out to be an appalling miscarriage of justice, Ferry was remanded in custody on charges of alleged witness nobbling. Gloucestershire police claimed that he had interfered with a witness in a case in which Otis was charged for allegedly taking a video camera from an anti-hunt protestor at a meet of the Heythrop. Charges against Ferry of attempting to pervert the course of justice were dropped after the police produced no evidence. But not until Ferry had spent four months in Gloucester prison. The judge described the police allegations as 'nonsense' and it was rumoured that the anti-hunting views of certain police officers, coupled with prodding from the Home Office, had led to Ferry's incarceration as a way of getting back at him for invading Parliament. In the end Ferry was given a one-year conditional discharge and fined £350 with £100 costs for causing 'fear, stress and upset' to a woman who tried to film him hunting. Hardly the stuff that sends you down.

With considerable understatement Ferry commented later, 'If you have ever been in prison you will know it is not very nice. I had to spend four months there for something I told the police was not true from day one.'

FROM HORACE TO FOOTBALL

'In the good old days a parson read Horace and rode to hounds.
Since agricultural depression has set in, the curate reads
Kipling and plays football.'

Old Etonian Irish baronet Sir John Leslie, from
The End of a Chapter, *1919.*
Diplomat and author Leslie, who wrote under the name of
Shane Leslie, was Sir Winston Churchill's first cousin.

THE ADVANTAGES OF A HUNT BALL

DRAGOONS OFFICER Colonel John Cook, writing in his 1826 book *Observations on Fox-Hunting*, claims that the hunt ball preesents a splendid opportunity for a shooting man to settle his differences with the hunt.

Cook tells the story of a country gent with three teenage daughters. Mama wishes to introduce them at the hunt ball but is worried they will not be welcome because her husband's keeper has shot every fox on the place.

She launches her attack at breakfast: 'It's very hard our poor girls cannot go to the hunt ball because of your nasty pheasants. You can't refuse them when I inform you that the eldest son of Sir G… R… Bart MP is to be there and you know he has lately paid some attention to our dear daughter Charlotte.'

Charlotte cuts in, 'Papa, you cannot be so unkind as to prevent me going to the *only* ball this winter.'

Sophia, second daughter, pipes up, 'My own dear Papa always said he was delighted when he saw his children happy. Pray, pray, pray, my own dear Papa, grant your affectionate child one great favour and that is to order old Killfox the keeper not to destroy any more foxes . Then we can go to the ball like our neighbours the Miss C….s.'

The women get their way. Papa's 'natural affection for his children prevailed over every other consideration and old Killfox, to his great amazement and mortification, was sent for and ordered to stay his hand and slay no more'.

Colonel Cook sums up this happy incident: 'The ladies went to the hunt ball in great glee and Miss Charlotte a few months after was married to the son of the Baronet. All was right and the advantages of a hunt ball very conspicuous.'

• Cook was a great raconteur. He told of a Frenchman out hunting one day. The man hadn't quite got the hang of things English. Hounds found a fox, but the creature failed to make much effort and the pack caught him immediately. The Frenchman rode up to Cook, took off his hat and exclaimed, 'Sir, I congratulate you on catching him so soon… and with so little trouble'.

• Cook had a desperate theory that wheat yields could be increased by a hunt riding over it. He wrote: 'In corn countries, it is usual for managers of fox-hounds to call out "ware wheat!" meaning, beware, don't ride over the wheat. It has however been often proved, that riding over wheat does it little injury, and farmers never have the least scruple in galloping over it themselves.'

• Shooting and hunting have always maintained an uneasy co-existence. The Edwardian hunting author C. F. P. McNeill could not have put it better when he wrote, 'In countries where there is shooting, a Master should write to each covert owner and ask him to kindly furnish the dates on which he intends to shoot, so that he may keep hounds out for the days previously, and also whether he would like hounds to come and cub-hunt his coverts. One sport should never be carried on to the detriment of another, and it must be remembered that there is no better sportsman than he who preserves foxes, though he is not a hunting man himself…'.

UNDER DRESSED?

THE DUKE OF WELLINGTON'S BALL in Paris in 1814 to celebrate Napoleon's abdication was attended by the young hunting-mad Marquess of Worcester and his wife. Worcester, later to become 6th Duke of Beaufort, wore the full Badminton Hunt garb: evening coat of blue lined with buff, a white embroidered silk waistcoat, tight light blue silk-web pantaloons, white silk stockings, shoes *brodes a jour,* and a cocked hat. A newspaper reporter at the event reassured us, 'Worcester never looked over-dressed'.

Note: back in those days the Badminton Hunt buttons were inscribed not with B.H. but with G.P.R. in deference to George, Prince Regent, 'first gentleman in Europe'.

FOXHUNTING AND RELIGION

The strangest place to give birth to cubs was a church in Heythrop country chosen by a vixen in July 1874. The vixen established her nursery in the Jacobean pulpit of eleventh century St Nicholas, Oddington, which was then derelict.

HOLIDAY FUN

The expression 'summer hunting' can be used as a euphemism for adulterous behaviour among the hunting community.

HUNTING AND FIGHTING

The Duke of Wellington kept a pack of hounds in Spain during the Peninsular War in order to amuse himself when he wasn't fighting the Frenchies. Wellington's officers thought this was frightfully good sport though the other ranks complained that the hounds were treated better than they were. The pack was given fresh meat while the soldiers fought on half-empty stomachs.

Wellington would ride in his light blue Hatfield Hunt frock coat, sent out to him by Lady Salisbury, one of his many female admirers. The field presented an awesome sight what with the dappled pack and the scarlet clad hunt servants amid the mass of red, green and blue army uniforms. Wellington preferred foxhunters on his staff to any other class of officer as they were so much better at carrying despatches across country. As someone remarked, 'Hunting one day and fighting the next – what more could a soldier possibly want?'

The huntsman was a Flintshire man called Tom Crane who had begun his career as a stable servant to Lt. Col. Sir Richard Puleston in a light dragoon regiment posted to Ireland during the 1798 rebellion. During a skirmish, Sir Richard's black mare called Priestess was shot dead under him. Crane, who was waiting in the rear with Sir Richard's second horse, became the hero of the day. Dodging enemy bullets, he dashed forward and rescued his master.

A year later Crane enlisted in the

Coldstream Guards ending up in the Peninsular as batman to Colonel John 'Jolly Jack' Fremantle, who happened to be Wellington's ADC. The Duke's foxhounds had just arrived from England and the big man needed somebody to hunt them.

Crane's earlier heroics paid off. Sir Richard Puleston, later to become Master of the Wynnstay in Cheshire, happened to know that Wellington was looking for a huntsman and recommended his former stable lad.

Wellington saw Crane's potential immediately. Crane was excellent with both hounds and horses and never without a smile on his face. 'His eyes were worth two of most other men's, and his ear was as true as his eye was quick', said a contemporary.

Wellington's hounds wound up the French something rotten. Crane and Wellington particularly enjoyed hunting behind enemy lines. 'Out of country', as Wellington put it. Napoleon's troops became used to the sound of Crane's hunting horn as he rode past them. The French soldiers watched open mouthed. They frequently took potshots at Crane. But not even the French would dare to shoot the hounds.

One day Crane went too far into enemy territory and was cut off by a patrol of French light cavalry. Their commanding officer came to the conclusion that the huntsman was not a threat. And his dogs were awfully nice. Crane and hounds were returned to British lines under a flag of truce.

When the Pensinsular War ended in 1814 Wellington discharged Crane from the army and gave him

SIR GILBERT? ON HAYNELL.

the job of running his stud at Hatfield, Hertfordshire. Crane married the daughter of the Marquis of Salisbury's steward and attempted to settle down. But he longed to be a huntsman again.

At the end of the war Wellington had given his hounds to Lord Stewart, better known as 'Fighting Charlie', one of his senior officers in the Peninsular. Stewart hunted with the Fife in Scotland. By 1821, the Fife had fallen on hard times. They had a useless huntsman and subscriptions had fallen off. Stewart asked Wellington if he could have Crane, the only man he knew who could sort things out. Wellington reluctantly let go of his favourite servant and Crane was back with his beloved pack at the Fife's kennels at Cupar.

The Fife country was so bare of foxes that Crane's first season produced fifteen blank days before Christmas. 'The hounds had become slack in the extreme', is how the hunting journalist Nimrod put it. 'But having learnt in the service of the Duke of Wellington to consider difficulties as trifles, Crane set to work, nothing daunted.'

Crane was a superb horseman. 'He rode with a peculiarly light hand, and had a curious, I might say unique, method of shaking the reins of his bridle, when going up to a large fence, which no doubt his horse knew the meaning of. He was a very quick man over country.'

Nimrod, ever the snob, added

that Crane was always so well turned he could have been born a gentleman: 'There was something in his general demeanour that would have led a stranger to suppose that there was a cross of good blood in his veins, that he was the son of a gentleman, instead of a gentleman's steward'.

Crane's career in Fife was tragically short. He died of pneumonia aged thirty-eight during the terrible winter of 1830. The hunt settled an exceptionally generous annuity of £50 per year on his widow.

• Sir Arthur Conan Doyle introduced Wellington's foxhounds into his *Exploits of Brigadier Gerard*, a fictitious officer in the French army. In one book, Gerard perpertrates the obscenity of shooting, in full view of the British field, a fox being hunted by Crane and his hounds.

• Despite the fuss, the Duke of Wellington was not a great catcher of foxes while in the Peninsular. Records reveal that his hounds killed only one fox in Portugal 1812-13. Nor was he a great horseman. Surtees (of Jorrocks fame) wrote, 'I have never seen a man with less idea of riding. His seat is unsightly in the extreme, and few men get more falls in the course of a year'.

• The Duke of Wellington's old garrison town of Pau, on the French side of the Pyrenees, still features a hunt. Le Pau Hunt, founded in 1840 by Napoleonic War veteran Sir Henry Oxenden, has not caught a fox since 1939 and has thus been reduced to following a drag.

SPORT OF A HIGHER ORDER

BISHOP SAMUEL WILBERFORCE was one of those Victorian clerics who saw nothing wrong with hunting and used every opportunity to introduce the subject into his services.

In 1850, while Bishop of Oxford, Wilberforce excelled himself with a sermon to a crowded congregation at St Michael's Church, off The Strand in London. He delivered 'an admirable discourse' on Judges 15, Verse 4 where Samson goes out and catches three hundred foxes.

'And excellent brave sport he must have had too!' cried the bishop. And with that he launched into an outrageous and entertaining lecture:

> 'I know, my brethren, that many look upon fox-hunting as a cruel and ungodly amusement, but I contend that fox-hunting is not cruel. Cock-fighting, I admit, is fraught with cruelty, because it is a cold-blooded act, witnessed by a few, principally of the lower orders, in places devoid of pomp and circumstance; but fox-hunting is surrounded by everything that can excite the mind and delight the senses. It is true that a panting, frightened fox is urged by howling dogs for hours, that, at length, weary and worn down by fatigue, it is caught, and torn limb from limb; it is true that horses and riders are maimed, while mothers, wives, and sisters, are sorrowfully anxious, not knowing who may be brought back from the field, a corpse or a mutilated sufferer; but, in spite of this, fox-hunting, as I have said before, is attended by so much excitement that it loses its traits of cruelty, and constitutes a sport of a higher order.'

Wilberforce, third son of anti-slavery campaigner William, is best remembered for his opposition to Charles Darwin's theory of evolution. In 1860 he participated in a debate with Darwin supporter, biologist Thomas Huxley. To the delight of the audience, the bishop asked Huxley whether it was through his grandfather or his grandmother that he claimed descent from a monkey.

Despite his warning about corpses being brought back from the hunting field, Wilberforce himself ended up a victim of a riding accident. He was killed instantly after being thrown from his horse on the Surrey downs in July 1873. Thomas Huxley got his own back by remarking that 'the bishop's brains had at last come into contact with reality, and the result had been fatal'.

'WARE SQUOILS

AN AMUSING 'TWO FINGERS' TO TONY BLAIR arrived in the days after the Hunting Ban in the form of the foundation of a new pack known as the Connaught Square Squirrel Hunt. Consisting of a terrier called Dillon and various mongrels of uncertain pedigree, the hunt was named after the leafy square in which the Prime Minister has his retirement residence.

The hunt was formed after Dillon's owner Edward Seyfried was walking the dog in Hyde Park when he chose to chase a squirrel. A policeman approached Mr Seyfried and cautioned him that under the new Hunting Act he could be fined £5,000, have his home searched and Dillon destroyed for allowing him to pursue a squirrel.

To circumvent the act, Mr Seyfried founded the Squirrel Hunt. The idea was that dog walkers could dress in full hunting kit while their dogs chased a smelly sock on the end of a length of string. More than 150 followers turned up at the first meet in Connaught Square.

'Taking Dillon on a drag hunt was the only legal way to take him for a walk in the park without keeping him on the lead,' Mr Seyfried explained. 'If he breaks away from the hunt and chases a squirrel instead of a sock, that's legal. It's so ridiculous.'

DISGUISED IN DRAG

THE WORLD'S only active military fox hunt claims to be the Fort Leavenworth, in Kansas, America. Soldiers began hunting with hounds in eastern Kansas soon after Fort Leavenworth was established in 1827. The organised hunt at Leavenworth was founded in 1926.

The truth is that despite making a big song and dance about their history and wearing red coats an' all, the Fort Leavenworth cannot be described as a proper hunt. They admit that hounds never actually kill anything. Instead their purpose is to give subscribers a 'unique hunting experience', whatever that may be.

OLD IDIOTS

THE LARGEST FUNERAL conducted for a single hound was in October 1859 when a harrier bitch called Old Glory was given a full-blown burial at Glossop, Derbyshire.

Old Glory, mother to no less than 175 pups, was said to possess extraordinary hunting skills. She was laid to rest in a coffin, her head surrounded by a hare's skin and bedecked by flowers. She was attended by several of her pups with black ribbons around their necks. Thousands of spectators crowded Glossop High Street as the funeral carriage passed. The huntsman blew a dirge on his horn at which the canine mourners set up a sympathetic howl.

Mourners were handed funeral cards bearing the inscription 'Sacred To The Memory of Glory Scholes', named after the hunt servant who had looked after her following her retirement from the pack. Mr Scholes had intended to deposit the creature's remains beneath a pear tree in his garden. But that was before members of the hunt intervened and insisted that such a fine hound should have a proper send off.

Not everyone approved of this mawkish ceremony. *Punch* Magazine made fun of the proceedings and described Old Glory's mourners as: 'the old idiots of Glossop – persons who may never be afraid of knocking out their brains in the hunting field'.

CENTAUR

GEORGE OSBALDESTON, Master of the Quorn and the Pytchley in the 1820s and 30s, was known as 'Squire' Osbaldeston because his neighbouring masters all possessed titles. Osbaldeston fell out badly with local farmers, who retaliated by shooting the Quorn's foxes. He was forced to take a standing order with Leadenhall Market in London for six bagged foxes per week.

Squire Osbaldeston rode with his stirrup leathers short like a jockey. He was a tiny man, no more than five feet, and eschewed the traditional top hat for a hunting cap as worn by hunt servants. 'He rode like a centaur, seeming to be almost part of his horse', commented a friend.

The mighty pace at which Osbaldeston rode and lived made him a legend. In one day with the Pytchley, he had three good runs, then hacked to Cambridge for a hunt ball, danced all night, rode back sixty miles, hunted the same day killing a a brace of foxes, and then rode fourteen miles home to dinner having not slept for two days.

• Having inherited little Osbaldeston attempted to support his hunting by entering sporting competitions, such as horse racing and pigeon shooting. He gambled furiously. Having made a small fortune in his youth, he lost his punter's knack in middle age. He died penniless aged eighty in 1866.

• Osbaldeston was an exceptional target shot. With a duelling pistol he put ten consecutive bullets on the ace of diamonds at a range of thirty feet.

• When Osbaldeston arrived at the Pytchley in 1827 after eight seasons with the Quorn, he declared, 'I have been in search of Paradise all my life, and have found it at last'.

GENTLEMAN ONLY

THE REV. BENJAMIN NEWTON, rector of a rural Yorkshire parish during the 1810s, kept a detailed diary, which included the pithy entry: 'Went hunting with Mr. Bell's hounds. Had tolerable sport. These hounds please me much as they are attended by gentlemen only. No farmers'.

PS AND QS

According to the Master of Foxhounds Association, on a hunting day the Master should:

Seek the landowner's or farmer's permission.

Be confident that he/she can recognise farmers by name on their own land.

Have knowledge of farm boundaries.

Have knowledge of how to cross the land.

Have some knowledge of individual farming practices such as lambing/calving dates.

Have preparations for cancelling, or delaying, meets because of inclement weather.

Also, MFHs should note the following:

Care must be taken on grass farms when it is wet especially in February and March.

With arable land, propose the use of headlands that help you to get through the farm easily which are acceptable to the farmer – stick to these throughout the season.

Arrangements for crossing one farm need to be tied in with those of adjoining farms.

During your visit arrange with the farmer how he wishes to be warned of a hunting day – card or telephone call. If you get on land unexpectedly, then give the relevant farmers a call.

Pony paddocks are ever increasing. When you are about your country, spot them, identify the owners and send them warning cards of when the hunt is about.

But most importantly, if there is a problem on a hunting day deal with it ASAP. And remember three words: PLEASE; THANK YOU; SORRY.

From Competencies Required Within A Mastership, *Master of Foxhounds Association.*

ONLY A WHITE ONE

One of the most unfortunate rows in the history of hunting happened in the years between the wars when some enterprising young Masters decided to liven up the English foxhound by crossing it with its Welsh counterpart. The two pioneers to experiment with Welsh outcrosses were Lt. Col. Sir Peter Farquhar (1904–1986) of the Meynell and Portman, and the half-American Isaac 'Ikey' Bell, (1880–1964) who had spent his early years hunting in Ireland before settling at the South and West Wilts.

Farquhar and Bell used, among other lines, the hounds of Monmouthshire landowner Sir Edward Curre to cross with their English stock. Sir Edward, regarded as Britain's greatest hound breeder, had been crossing English bitches with Welsh stallions since the end of the nineteenth century. He had produced a fast hound without the traditional hairy Welsh coat. His pack was white 'so I could see them in the distance'.

Writing in *Horse & Hound* many years later, Farquhar explained his actions: 'Up to the 1914–18 war came a sad period in the history of the foxhound. Their breeding got into the hands of a few influential Masters who did not hunt their own hounds, but bred for fashion and the show ring. They created what was

later to be known as the "Peterborough" type. They wanted a hound to be very big, very wide through the chest, which of course put the elbows out, and to have tremendous bone...Such hounds were nothing more nor less than cripples; they could not gallop nor had they much inclination to hunt. The unfortunate Hunt servants had to do the hounds'work for them, which is why galloping about all over the countryside (interpreted as brilliant casts) became the normal practice in fashionable countries. A few English packs, notably the Heythrop, Berkeley and Brocklesby, resisted this fashion, but of course their breeding policy became very limited and difficult'.

Bell added that hound breeders had been so concerned by looks that light coloured hound whelps were being destroyed at birth because they weren't the 'right colour'. When he visited kennels, huntsmen would frequently keep back their light-coloured hounds because they were embarrassed by them. 'I remember a young man, after being severely spoken to by the master for kicking a hound, excusing himself on the ground that it was 'only a white one'!'

Bell was convinced that the best performing hounds were not necessarily the best lookers. 'I once heard an old master say that more foxes are lost at Peterborough than in any other place. To these people, the gaily coloured Bramham Moor

with their superb backs and shoulders fell from grace; the Brocklesby knees were faulted, and the Warwickshire were pronounced light and wanting in rib. Milton was criticised for having too much white in the kennel, and the Fitzhardinge...became relegated to oblivion. I have even heard surprise expressed that the ancestral pye colour of the Badminton still was found in that Ducal pack!'

Farquhar and Bell argued that the English hound was suffering from severe inbreeding and urgently needed new blood in the form of the sleek and hairy Welshman. But their actions provoked incredible anger amongst the English hunting community. They were treated as pariahs and outcasts. Country gents would cross the road in London if either man was coming their way; they were subjected to verbal abuse in their clubs. MFHs throughout England cursed the pair for the Welsh invasion.

Their opponents said they were quite wrong to say that the Peterborough type was too slow. A *Horse & Hound* correspondent calling himself 'Old Time Hunt Servant' accused the new breed of hound as resembling a lurcher. They were 'crooked, back at the knee, with feet like an Alsatian and hocks back in the next parish. For goodness sake, Masters and judges, come away from these Greyhound-Alsatian types...Hunting is hunting, not coursing'.

Last word to Sir Peter: 'People sometimes tell me that they think the modern foxhound is too fast, but it is not the pace at which they can gallop that matters – it is the pace at which they hunt…it is the fast, intelligent, hard-driving packs of hounds which show sport, and catch foxes, day in and day out, throughout the season. And long may they continue to do so'.

• Isaac 'Ikey' Bell was an Old Harrovian of independent means , the son of an American heiress. He spent thirty years with hounds and is considered as the man who gave us the modern foxhound. By the early 1930s, badly crippled with arthritis, he attempted to continue hunting by riding side saddle, but was forced to give up. Now describing himself as a 'non-hunting man', he turned instead to ocean racing, becoming the first American to be elected to the Royal Yacht Squardon. Like everything Bell did in life he was determined to be the best. He became a celebrated yachtsman, famed for building the 1936 Camper and Nicholson Fastnet Race winner *Bloodhound*, later bought by the Queen.

• Ikey Bell had five nuggets of advice for a prospective Master of Foxhounds:

1. Hounds will know more about hunting than you will.
2. The secret of success for a pack of hounds is condition.
3. The most important trait to inspire a young hound is trust.
4. Should some mistakes ever cause you to deceive hounds, you must spare no trouble in making it up to them.
5. Hounds have sharp hearing and they dont like to be shouted at as if they were deaf!

A Huntsman's Log Book, *Eyre and Spottiswode, London, 1947*

LIGHTBULB JOKE

Q: How many cubhunters does it take to change a lightbulb?

A: If you'd laid out your kit the night before you wouldn't need to worry about the lightbulb.

POP TRIVIA

'And who is the master of foxhounds
And who says the hunt is begun
And who calls the tune in the court-room
And who beats the funeral drum.'

From 'Free Four', the fifth track on Pink Floyd's 1972 album Obscured by Clouds, one of the few rock lyrics to mention foxhounds. With the ban in mind, were these prophetic words? The song was written by the Floyd's Roger Waters, a keen shooting man, who has made no secret of his support for hunting. The lyrics are said to deal with the death of his father, who followed hounds with the Zetland.

WOT WILL IT COST?

MOST FAMOUS FICTITIOUS FOXHUNTER IS JORROCKS, the cockney sportsman created by the Victorian writer Surtees in his book *Handley Cross*. Robert Smith Surtees (1805–64) was a country gent from County Durham who began 'scribbling', as he put it, after getting bored training as a solicitor. He replaced Charles Apperley – aka Nimrod – as hunting correspondent at the *Sporting Magazine* in 1830.

But Surtees was not a patch on his predecessor and was sacked a year later. He launched a rival publication with the unimaginative title *The New Sporting Magazine* where he wrote a series of caricatures about a hunting parvenu called Jorrocks.

Surtees fleshed out the Jorrocks stories into his debut novel *Handley Cross*, published in 1843. After a slow start the book became a best seller, praised by greats like Thackeray and Kipling.

In *Handley Cross*, Jorrocks is an exceptionally common City tea merchant. In his own words he is a 'Post 'Hoffice Directory not a Peerage man' who rides with the Surrey Hunt, near Croydon. His personifies the new hunting, that by the 1840s is open to all. 'Tell me a man's foxhunter and I loves 'im'. He seldom jumps, preferring to trot. His nemesis is Pomponious Ego, a hunting journalist (based on Nimrod), who is invited to the spa town of Handley Cross where Jorrocks has taken a pack of hounds.

The hunting is a disaster, not least because James Pigg the huntsman is hunting with an aniseed drag. Jorrocks, who consumes two pints of port per night, has difficulty staying on his horse, and dismounts at jumps, pulling his nag over while shouting at it. To his credit Jorrocks knows the country well and believes that hounds are more important than riding. He describes the practise when hounds stop running because the scent gives out as 'throwing up'. But he explains, 'This doesn't mean womitin' mind, but standin' starin' with their 'eads up, instead of keepin' them down, tryin' for the scent'.

Jorrocks knows that the only reason he is accepted as an MFH is because he has money. (Where have we heard that before?) He explains, 'I'm a sportsman all over, and to the backbone. – 'Unting is all that's worth living for – all time is lost wot is not spent in 'unting – it is like the hair we breathe...'. but 'enough of the rhapsodies, let us come to the melodies – the £ s. d. in fact. Wot will it cost?'

At the end of the book, Jorrocks' London friends have him committed to a lunatic asylum to prevent him spending more money on the hunt thereby saving his fortune. Jorrocks is eventually released and the story ends with him preparing for another season.

HUNTING AS RELIGION

The most bizarre opposition to the 2004 Hunting Act came in the form of a new church specially established as a way of getting around the ban.

The founders of the Free Church of Country Sports claimed that foxhunting was part of their religion and that legislation to ban it was an infringement of their rights.

They were helped by the fact that Labour's animal welfare minister Ben Bradshaw claimed priggishly that the ban was brought in out of respect for 'the religious freedoms and fundamental beliefs of people in this country'.

The organisers of the new church pounced on this and pointed to the Government's decision to allow the ritual slaughter of animals by Jews and Muslims because a ban would discriminate against religious groups.

Church 'founding father' Rod Brammer, owner of a Devon shooting school, claimed that hunting had numerous comparisons with established religions. 'We have our own language and our own art. Those in the Jewish faith blow a horn, the shofar, and so do we. Hunting is a form of ritualised killing – in our case the odds of actual killing are stacked in favour of the animal to escape. We baptise our children by blooding them with the blood of that which we kill. Is this any more strange than dressing them

in white and totally submerging them in water?'

Despite an initial flurry of interest the Church of Country Sports never took off. It was left to more secular groups, such as the Countryside Alliance and the Conservative Party, to oppose the ban.

• The Free Church of Country Sports's muse was Saint Hubert, the seventh century Belgian patron saint of hunters. Before he found his faith Hubert was a nobleman who enjoyed hunting. One Good Friday morning, while everybody else was in church, he was on his horse enjoying a marvellous run in the forests of the Ardennes. As he pursued his stag he saw a vision of a crucifix standing between its antlers, accompanied by a voice telling him that he was destined for hell unless he turned to God. Hubert gave up the sport and went into the church. He spent years doing missionary work in the forests where had once hunted.

FIRST LADY

FIERCE HUNTING LADY MARY AMELIA CECIL, Marchioness of Salisbury, was England's first lady Master. A incorrigibly fast rider, she took over the Mastership of the Hatfield Hunt after her husband's death in 1793.

Under Lady Salisbury's Mastership, the kennels moved to Hatfield House. She led the field dressed in sky-blue habit with black collar and cuffs. Despite oncoming blindness, she continued hunting into her seventies. She could still exhaust riders half her age. At the end of her life she had to be taken out on a lead reign. At every jump her groom would shout, ' Damn you, my lady, jump!'

Lady Salisbury died aged 85 in 1835 in a fire that destroyed the west wing of Hatfield House.

> • The emergence of women in the hunting field in the eighteenth century caused great consternation. The Scottish poet James Thomson (1700–48) expressed his unease about lady foxhunters in his poem *The Seasons*:

> But if the rougher sex by this fierce sport
> Is hurried wild, let not such horrid joy
> E'er stain the bosom of the British Fair.
> Far be the spirit of the chase from them;
> Uncomely courage, unbeseeming skill;
> To spring the fence, to rein the prancing steed;
> The cap, the whip, the masculine attire,
> In which they roughen to the sense, and all
> The winning softness of their sex is lost.

HUNT THE BARMAN

WHEREVER THE BRITISH ARMY WENT there was foxhunting, or at least a vague attempt at it. During the Second World War, officers stationed at the Hotel Baron, in Aleppo, Syria, an old haunt of Lawrence of Arabia, would practice foxhunting around the corridors. The part of the fox was played by a long-suffering barman called Yezegel who allowed himself to be chased in return for a good tip . The hotel bar is said to have made a splendid bullfinch.

EARLY START

HUNTING IN ENGLAND at the turn of the nineteenth century meant rising from your bed while it was still dark. Colonel John Cook, hunting writer and Master of the Essex 1808-1813, suggested that the sunrise meet was adopted with the specific purpose of hunting Charlie while he was still half asleep, stiff and unbreakfasted. Otherwise hounds, which tended to be slower in those days, would never catch him. By the late 1820s, hound breeding had revolutionised the sport. Cook wrote in 1829, 'The breed of hounds, the feeding, and the whole system is so much improved that the majority of foxes are found and killed after twelve o'clock'.

EXACTING, TROUBLESOME AND IMPERIOUS

'There are two classes of women who ride to hounds...There is the lady who rides, and demands assistance; and there is the lady who rides, and demands none. The lady who rides and demands assistance in truth becomes a nuisance before the run is over, let her beauty be ever so transcendent, her horsemanship ever so perfect, and her battery of general feminine artillery ever so powerful. She is like the American woman, who is always wanting your place in a railway carriage, and demanding it, too, without the slightest idea of paying you for it with thanks... The hunting lady who demands assistance is very particular about her gates, requiring that aid shall be given to her with instant speed, but that the man who gives it shall never allow himself to be hurried as he renders it. It is marvellous to watch the manner in which a hunting lady will become exacting, troublesome, and at last imperious, deceived and spoilt by the attention which she receives. She teaches herself to think at last that a man is a brute who does not ride as though he were riding as her servant...'

From Hunting Sketches *by Anthony Trollope 1865*

THE UNDOMESTICATED FOXHUNTER

Young ladies frequently asked the Victorian hunting journalist Robert Smith Surtees whether they would be more likely to find a husband if they took up foxhunting. This was his reply:

'Be cautious. It may catch him, or it may scare him. Some men...would rather have a wife staying at home looking after the house than tearing about the country after the hounds. Besides, it is possible you might beat him, and men don't like being beat by their wives in the field, any more than wives like being beat by their husbands in the house.'

In an article for the sporting paper *Bell's Life in London,* Surtees tells the story of Henrietta Cottonwool who has been after Sir Rasper Smashgate 'the whole of this blessed season, and now, as spring is about to set in, with its usual severity, she feels herself constrained to take some decided step'.

Henrietta is a 'fine, large, full-grown, healthy-looking girl' who will do anything to snare a husband.

The hopes and fears of Smashers, as his friends call him, are limited to 'his stud with the addition, perhaps, of his razors. If he got a good shave in the morning he was generally happy for the rest of the day, for he had twelve as good hunters as a sixteen stone man could desire, with two thorough-bred hacks, and a stud-groom equal to his business, and yet not above it'.

To cut a long story short, Henrietta's pushy mother Mrs Cottonwool invites Sir Rasper to dinner. But on the day of the dinner Sir Rasper is hunting the other side of the county and the invitation slips his mind. He never turns up, preferring to eat at a country pub with the rest of the muddy field.

Henrietta and Mama are outraged. Mrs C puts it down 'as a case of desertion'. Her daughter should have nothing more to do with Sir Rasper since it is 'impossible to look for conjugal happiness with a man so thoroughly undomesticated'.

At this point Henrietta's father Mr Cottonwool chips and says 'that he never thought there was anything in it'. His wife tells him to 'hold his tongue, and not talk about things he does not understand'.

Henrietta is determined to have another shot at Smashers. She contrives to bump into him on the way to the season's final meet...

Henrietta is a fine looking girl, but on the plump side. 'She is a good load (on her horse), though her well-formed back and waist are admirably developed by the close-fitting evenness of her well-made London habit'.

Smashgate bears down the road 'like a man-of-war in full sail. He comes at the pace of the regular five or six days a week man, who knows to a minute how long it will take him to 'do' each meet'.

He greets Henrietta with 'the hearty cordiality of a half-way-met agreeably-surprised foxhunter. He is pleased with the attention of so fine a girl. A tinge of pink pervades Henrietta's bright healthy complexion, as she recognises the pressure of his somewhat hard hand'.

Smashgate continues to the meet.

But the seed is sown. Surtees writes triumphantly, 'It is clear there must be a first thought, a first impulse as to marrying a girl, and Sir Rasper's impulse came on him rather suddenly this morning. Pleased with Henrietta's appearance, flattered by her preference, and perhaps wanting a solace for the fast wearing-out season, he says to himself as he changes his hack for his hunter, 'By Jove, why shouldn't I marry her?'

THREE TYPES OF FOXHUNTER

'There are three descriptions of men who go out hunting:

The first see the hounds;
The second see those who see the hounds;
The third see nothing at all'.

The Sporting Magazine, *1825*

NO JOKES

Should hunt servants be seen but not spoken to? Heed this advice from Reginald Monckton, Master of the Albrighton Hounds in the 1930s and author of a jolly little booklet called *Hunting Reflections*. Note that this was written for the children of the Albrighton Hunt Pony Club in the hope that they would avoid becoming too familiar with the flunkeys:

- The Hunt servants are the Master's personal servants, and should be treated as you would your host's servants when in a friend's house.

- It is infra dig to crack jokes with them and incorrect to talk to them unless you have information to convey to them.

- They have their work to do all the time they are hunting in looking after hounds, and if you talk to them you distract their attention from their duty.

- Always give the Whips precedence at jumps, as they have to be there to do their work, and their horses have far harder work than yours.

> • Reggie Monckton's son Alan, a Staffordshire squire, recalls that his father took him hunting as a boy on a pony called Winter Boy, said to be the grandson of a Derby winner. One day while out with the North Staffs, Monckton younger cut up a lady at a brook. 'Just as I jumped I heard a loud female voice behind me and looked back to see the Master's wife who had been forced to stop abruptly before the stream'. Monckton saw his father a few minutes later. He related what had happened and chirruped innocently, 'She shouted two words at me which I haven't heard before. What do they mean?' His father blushed. The incident evidently had a marked effect on Monckton. He is now resolutely a shooting man.

A FINE THING

'It would be a fine thing for many a country squire if he loved his neighbours as much as he loved his pack of hounds.' From a sermon by the Rev. Charles Haddon Spurgeon, 1858. Spurgeon was a London Baptist churchman who preached up to ten sermons a week . Known as the 'Prince of Preachers' he is said to have preached to ten million people during his lifetime. Spurgeon loved hunting and littered his sermons with references to the noble science.

PEACHES AND CHAMPAGNE

THE MODERN HUNTING BOOT was designed by Regency fashion fop Beau Brummell, who created the white tops that were to become de rigeur in the shires. Brummel polished his boots with blacking mixed with peaches and champagne. His fashion maxim was that the best dressed man in the hunting field was the man whose attire attracted least notice.

WHIPPED OFF

During the 1930s the Berkeley Hunt had a hound
called Whipcord, which had suffered the
indignity of having only half a tail,
the missing half having being
bitten off by a rat.

STRONG LADY

'A BAD DAY'S SPORT IN LEICESTERSHIRE is better than a good day in the provinces.' Lady Augusta Fane, fearless Edwardian hunting lady.

'Gussy' Fane had firm views on hunting. She deplored girls who considered it 'early Victorian to study anything'. Few mastered the art of horsemanship. She told the story of a girl who fell off and was rescued by the Master who said she might be more secure if she shortened her stirrups two holes and sat in the centre of her saddle. The girl replied, 'Thank you, but we don't ride like that, it's quite out of date'. Later in the day she was carted off with a broken collar bone.

Lady Augusta (1880–1950), daughter of the 2nd Earl of Stradbroke, was the prettiest debutante of her generation. Her autobiography, titled *Chit-Chat,* excelled on the subject of hunting, though many thought it would have been a lot better had she revealed details of her love affairs which were numerous. But that would have been considered terribly vulgar in 1926.

NEVER FLY TRENCHED CELERY

Tongue in cheek advice for huntsmen tempted to pursue the fox into somebody's garden:

• It is extremely tiring to horse and man to ride the cucumber beds at right angles...always proceed as with any other ridge and furrow. Trenched celery can be really dangerous. It should never be flown, but negotiated with all the care and caution called for by the big Meath ditches.

• Box hedges look very tempting, but they have to be jumped (i.e. rather than ridden through). Many a man who thought he was jumping a box hedge has found (too late) that he was jumping the early violets as well. The take off should be a good five feet from the hedge, or a hind leg may be dropped into the glass-topped violet frame. If you have broken the violet frame, you will have spoilt the pleasure of some other person who wants to jump it.

• A lawn tennis court can be ridden just as you would ride a golf green, but those tiresome hard courts can interrupt your galloping progress.

• A half-grown yew hedge makes a delightful obstacle, but if the hedge is higher than a wheelbarrow it should be jumped at some point where the yews are a little backward. Gardeners have a trick of leaving wheelbarrows behind hedges and will sometimes even fill them with flower pots. A nasty fall may result. When you next ride that way the wheelbarrow may have been removed, but the gardener may be there with an offer to 'give you all the flower pots you want'. There can be no harm in charging down a herbaceous border scattering those plants name tags on sticks. This can be similar sport to tent pegging.

• Galloping through chicken runs can be done in the spirit of your cock-fighting ancestors. Make sure you have wire cutters with you.

From Hunting Lore, *by 'Crascredo and The Wag', Country Life Books, 1928*

THE KEEN FOXHUNTER'S MISCELLANY

LANDOWNER AND PROPHET

The final quarter of the nineteenth century saw an increasing number of attacks on field sports from left-wingers. A spirited writer was needed to trash the opposition. Step forward William Bromley-Davenport, Conservative MP and Cheshire landowner – motto: 'Hunt and be happy' – who was determined to show up the shortcomings of the anti-bloodsporters.

Bromley-Davenport's 1885 volume simply entitled *Sport* is one of the most entertaining field sports books ever written. He used it to launch into a tirade against anyone trying to meddle with his beloved hunting. Such people were no better than 'a saturnalia of prigs' immersed in an 'apotheosis of claptrap'.

'Legislation has performed such queer antics lately that the angels must be beginning to weep', wrote the peppery B-D, referring to the 1880 Ground Game Act which gave tenant farmers the right to shoot vermin, including foxes. He foresaw a bad time for hunting in Britain: 'Ugly visions haunt me of a time coming, which shall be a good time to no man, at least to no Englishman, when an impossible standard of pseudo-philanthropy and humanitarian morality shall be attempted; when the butcher shall lie down with the lamb, the alderman with the turtle, and the oyster shall not be eaten without anaesthetics; when nature itself shall be under the eye of the police, and detectives watch the stoat's pursuit of the rabbit and keep guard over spiders' webs... when, as a final climax to our national madness, we have employed science to dig a hole under the sea, and, by connecting us with the Continent, deprive us of the grand advantage which nature has given us, and which has conferred on us centuries of envied stability, while thrones were rocking and constitutions sinking all around us.'

• Victorian cynics such as Bromley-Davenport observed that the most vociferous anti was the middle-class woman who had hunted in her youth and then lost her nerve. Having given up, she tried to justify her lack of courage with a self-righteous anger towards a sport she had once loved. 'When women lose their nerve, they found out as hunting is cruel,' is how one old hand put it.

PRIORITIES

THE NOVELIST JOHN MASTERS described a yeomanry colonel he met during the Second World War in the 1941 Iraq campaign. The fellow had a dreadful memory and had difficulty remembering his officers' names. During an inspection, the colonel went down the line introducing his officers to a visitor. Masters wrote, 'He stopped before one captain, and said, "This is Captain…Captain…" He shook his head, snapped his fingers and cried genially, "Memory like a sieve! I'll be forgetting the names of me hounds next".'

BETTER THAN MOST

'Bounding o'er brook with gallant air,
Magennis comes in view,
Who rides with single arm to hounds
Better than most with two.'

Anonymous homily to Major Dick Magennis, of the Oakley Hunt, who lost his arm at the Battle of Albuera (Peninsular War), 1811

SCENT

Anyone who knows anything about hunting will consider this information superfluous, possibly insulting. But weekend foxhunter-commuters need to know that a fox's scent comes from its pads and not from its fur. You can prove this by rubbing yourself with the pad of a newly-killed fox. The stink will still be on you when you're back in your office the next week.

FLIT FLOP

FIRST EXAMPLE OF HUNT SABOTEURS AT WORK happened in August 1958 when members of the League Against Cruel Sports used chemicals to disrupt the Devon and Somerset Staghounds. They made a big fuss of the fact that they deployed a 'secret' concoction , although it was probably nothing more exciting than fox pee. The League claimed a great victory. But the Devon and Somerset's Master, Colonel Murphy, declared the incident a frightful flop: 'It was a normal day's hunting from every point of view – including the fact that we did not catch a stag'.

The hunt realised that dirty tricks were afoot when a vehicle carrying a weed sprayer was seen sprinkling the roadside. This had little effect on the pack, which behaved perfectly.

Colonel Murphy, a buffer of the old school, could not conceal his contempt for the antis. 'They only had a Flit gun, the sort of thing we used in India to keep the mosquitoes off. The hounds paid no attention to it whatsoever.'

WHAT ONE DOES

When asked by a visitor what one did in Meath in the summer,
Daisy, Countess of Fingall, (1865–1944), matriarch of
one of Ireland's great hunting families,
replied, 'We wait for the winter'.

NOT ENOUGH HUNTING

GEORGE V must have regretted the day he told his seventeen-year-old son Prince Edward, the future Edward VIII, that he was doing 'too much shooting, and not enough riding or hunting'.

Papa, a keen horseman, urged in a letter, 'You must learn to ride and hunt properly. In your position it is absolutely necessary that you should ride well. The English people like riding and it would make you very unpopular if you couldn't do so. If you can't ride, you know, I'm afraid people will call you a duffer.'

It was 1912. The Prince of Wales had left Naval College and gone up to Oxford. There he was assigned an equerry who would teach him to ride. Soon he was playing polo. He then joined the South Oxfordshire Hounds. And all was lost…

Edward became utterly obsessed by hunting. He took rooms in Melton Mowbray and hunted several days a week, regardless of academic commitments. He had a flat in Craven Lodge and the drawing room was littered with pictures of his horses including his favourite hunter Miss Muffit. His horses became his children. Once when one of his hunters developed palpitations he took the animal not to a vet but to a heart specialist.

King George tried to back track. 'You certainly have been doing a good deal, hunting two days, out with the beagles twice, golf and shooting one day, besides all your work…I hope you are not over-doing it…'

To his father's horror Edward decided that even more fun than hunting was racing. He began to enter point-to-points. He rode in many races and had several wins.

Edward's equestrian adventures went down hill in 1924 when he broke his collar bone while exercising one of his hunters near Leighton Buzzard in preparation for a day with the Whaddon Chase. The prince remounted his horse thinking he had done no damage. His equerry Captain Metcalfe remarked, 'I think your collar-bone is broken, sir'. The prince shrugged his shoulders and winced. 'I believe it is,' he replied.

On 15 March Edward fell badly at the Army Point-to-Point at Arborfield Cross, Berkshire. Both Edward and his brother Prince Henry, later Duke of Gloucester, had competed in two races. In the last race, the Past and Present Steeplechase for Lord Cavan's Cup, Edward made a balls up of a fence and fell. He was kicked in the face and ended up in bed at St James's Palace for three weeks with concussion. Observers noted that the horse, a bay gelding called Little Favourite, had been No. 13 on the card and carrying 13 stone. Most unlucky.

The Press claimed the future monarch was putting himself in too much danger. They said he was a hopeless rider, continually falling off. Not so different to Prince Charles's Press treatment in his accident-prone polo playing days.

Letters appeared in the papers saying Edward should quit. Prime Minister Ramsay MacDonald asked him to tone down his riding. He took no notice and continued to race and hunt furiously. It was only in 1928 when the King fell ill that Edward finally gave up. His mother Queen Mary asked him to stop racing and stick to hunting. But racing had become his great love and hunting was second best. In a fit of pique, he sold his horses and surrendered his digs at Melton. A few months later he met Wallis Simpson. Perhaps things would have turned out better had he stuck to horses.

Last word to George V. In frustration at his heir's racecourse escapades, he asked nobody in particular: 'Why doesn't my son ride like a gentleman?'

• Prince Henry came a cropper at the same Army Point-to-Point in 1924. He was riding Rathgarogue in the Nomination Race . The horse refused the second fence, swerved, and, in the words of The Times, 'became mixed up with a bicycle'. Horse and rider came down but no injury done except for minor abrasions to both. Bicycle well and truly buggered.

• Edward first met Wallis Simpson while he was hunting at Melton Mowbray. Edward was staying in a house party at Burrough Court, the country home of his latest mistress Lady Furness. Wallis, suffering from a dreadful cold, was also a guest. Knowing that she was about to meet Royalty for the first time, Wallis had spent much of the train journey from London learning how to curtsy.

ODORIFEROUS QUARRY

The lamentable earthiness of the Germans is illustrated by a story told by Irish politician Valentine, 2nd Baron Cloncurry during his European tour of 1805.

Cloncurry stayed for a week's hunting with Prince Xavier of Saxony at Schloss Zabelditz, a few miles from Dresden. 'There I partook of the old German princely hospitality in its most unsophisticated shape', his lordship recalled in his memoirs. When the weather allowed, the party 'hunted the boar in great force'. Otherwise, it was a fairly steady week.

One day it rained so heavily that the party were forced to remain indoors. Cloncurry's heart sank for the company was dull in the extreme. It was the sort of stodgy house party you might expect during a wet week in Saxony.

Much to Cloncurry's astonishment, the day was enlivened by his princely host determined to show his fun side.

Cloncurry recalled, 'The tedium of the long afternoon was relieved by the introduction of a couple of boar hounds the largest dogs I ever saw into the dining hall to hunt a bagged polecat'.

One only imagines the chaos. Apart from anything else, the smell of a polecat after several hours in a bag must have been dreadful.

Cloncurry pointed out that the creature's fate was unimportant. Much more fun was the effect of two boarhounds running amok among the furniture, onto which had clambered the female guests. 'The chief zest of the sport was the terror of the ladies and their efforts to avoid the enormous dogs and their odoriferous quarry by jumping upon chairs and tables as they approached.'

HAS HUNTED

Advice from *Horse & Hound* magazine for when you see that perfect hunter advertised in the classifieds…

1. Many failed competition horses are re-sold as 'hunters'. This is not always a good thing as the fault that ended their competitive career can sometimes reappear on the hunting field.

2. If you buy a horse at a sale and he was advertised as a 'good hunter', you would have legal redress if he acted up the first time he saw hounds.

3. If a horse is advertised as having hunted with a particular pack, ask hunt members if he is known to them.

4. Some horse dealers specialise in hunters and you could save yourself a lot of time and money by going to this type of yard to find your horse. The horse dealer will be able to assess the kind of horse you need, and he should be able to offer a selection for you to try.

5. Do not expect to be allowed a day's hunting as a trial. Few sellers, private or trade, will let a stranger take a horse out hunting because of the obvious risks to horse and rider.

6. The best way to buy a hunter is through recommendation. If a horse you like isn't being openly advertised, it's always worth asking the owner if they would be prepared to sell.

7. When you buy a hunter privately always get some sort of statement in writing, or verbally in front of a witness. Ask clearly whether the horse has hunted, how often and with which pack. In case of problems later this can be presented in court and you would have a good case if there has been deliberate misrepresentation by the seller.

8. Do not expect a horse that has only hunted quietly with a slow pack to tackle Leicestershire hedges confidently on your first outing together.

9. Do not be swayed by flashy looks when you buy a hunter. The aim is to enjoy your sport and the best-looking hunters are not always the safest ones.

10. Unless you are an experienced rider, it is better to go for an older horse with some miles on the clock. It takes skill and knowledge to introduce a young horse to hounds and, if this is done badly, the repercussions will stay to haunt you.

Author's note: Adopt extreme caution when you see the words 'has hunted' in a classified ad. This can mean that the horse went hunting once but behaved so badly that it was never allowed out again…

PITCHED BATTLE

One of the biggest jeers ever received by a Member of
Parliament was given to the Radical statesman John
Bright who during a debate on the Corn Laws referred
to the Pytchley Hunt as the 'Pitchley'. That an MP could not
pronounce the name of one of Britain's most famous hunts was
considered inexcusable. In the Pytchley's annals it was later
written, 'Honourable members seemed astonished that one of
their number, and that so distinguished one as the senior
member for Birmingham, should be ignorant of the proper
mode of pronouncing the name of this well-known hunt… Mr
Bright had probably never seen a pack of hounds in the field. To
him the Quorn, the Pytchley, and the Cottesmore, are
institutions unworthy the notice of any rightly thinking man,
and great must have been his surprise at finding that so small an
error had raised so great a laugh'.

MAY GALLOPS ADD YEARS TO YOUR LIFE

'I was much amused a few seasons ago by a traveller in
the grocery business, who contrived to take his country
rounds for orders on horseback, and also contrived that
his journeys should be made in the direction and on the
days when hounds met. How that man enjoyed himself,
and how often he was blown up for being in the very
place he should not have been, yet I could have taken
my hat off to him. A sportsman in practice he certainly
was not, yet I much doubt if, out of the three or four
hundred men who four times in the week met those
hounds, a truer one at heart could have been found. I
trust his gallops may add years to his life, as most likely
they will. Here was a man with no more chance of
pursuing any other sport than he had of becoming
prime minister…No one sport brings all classes together
like the chase, except perhaps the cricket field.'

From Covert-Side Sketches *by J. Nevill Fitt, 1879*

HOLY FOX

LORD HALIFAX was one of the most remarkable foxhunters of the twentieth century. Despite having been born with a withered left arm with no hand, he never allowed the disability to affect his riding. He rode to hounds from an early age and joined the cavalry in the First World War.

As a young man Halifax said, 'I would rather be a Master of Foxhounds than premier'. He realised his first ambition in 1932 when he was chosen Master of the Middleton in Yorkshire. He held the post until 1938 when pressures of public life forced him to give it up.

Halifax was one of the most senior Conservative politicians of the 1930s and 40s. He is regarded as one of the architects of appeasement prior to the Second World War, famous for acting on behalf of the British government in an attempt to renew dialogue with the German government. In November 1937, Hermann Goering invited Halifax to Germany on the pretext of a trip to Pomerania for a fox shoot. One can only imagine the reaction of the Master of the Middleton when suggested to him that he might like to shoot foxes. The word apoplexy comes to mind.

Halifax turned down the Pomeranian invitation with the excuse that he had a bad shoulder. Instead he visited a hunting exhibition in Berlin before being entertained at Goering's country estate Karinhall. Two days later Halifax was in Berchtesgarten meeting Adolph Hitler. The meeting was not a success, not least because upon arriving at Hitler's mountain lair he mistook the Fuhrer for a footman and almost passed him his bowler hat. Hitler spent the time raging against the inefficiency of Europe's democracies and Halifax left Germany having achieved little.

At the end of the war Halifax couldn't wait to resume his Mastership of the Middleton. He is said to have made a tremendous success of hunting hounds in the Wednesday and Saturday country.

• Winston Churchill nicknamed Halifax the 'Holy Fox' in reference to both his devout Anglo-Catholicism and his love of the chase. Hermann Goering nicknamed him Halali, after a German hunting call.

SENTIMENTALISTS MASQUERADING AS HEROES

'Anybody who was really disturbed by animal suffering would be far more troubled by the practice of poisoning rats than by that of hunting foxes. But rats do not look right. A fox's mask resembles the face of an alert and interesting human; the face of a rat is sneaky and full of intrigue, while its colour, legs and tail belong to a subterranean world which to us is the world of the tomb. The fox therefore provides a suitable object for those pretend emotions through which sentimentalists fortify their image of themselves as heroes of compassion.'

From Animal Rights and Wrongs *by philosopher Roger Scruton, Demos, 1996*

BUMPKINS AND BOOBIES

HUNTING WAS INTRODUCED TO ITALY In 1836 by the Tory politician, George Stanhope, 6th Earl of Chesterfield.

George went to Italy with his wife Anne to cure her lung problems. Bored of kicking around in Rome with nothing to do, he ordered his fox hounds to be sent from England. When he returned home he left the pack behind so that the locals could be educated in the noble science. Thankfully, Chesterfield inherited none of his great-grandfather's prejudice towards English hunting. The 4th Earl of Chesterfield, known as a great man of letters, complained, 'The French manner of hunting is gentleman-like; ours is only for bumpkins and boobies'.

CHUCK UP CHARLIE

THE 1796 EDITION of a London publication titled *A Classical Dictionary Of The Vulgar Tongue* reveals that in hunting circles the vulgar pronunciation of the French words 'faux pas' is translated into 'fox's paw', as in, 'He made a confounded fox's paw of it'. The same book tells us that the expression 'to flay the fox' means to vomit.

NO TRAMPLING

Baily's Sporting Magazine reported in 1869 the four principle 'crimes' that make people 'do mischief with hounds':

1. Overriding and pressing hounds
2. Heading foxes
3. Forging ahead and speculating
4. Cutting off hounds.

The four reasons for committing these atrocities were:

1. Jealousy
2. Anxiety
3. Nervousness
4. Ignorance.

The worst crime of all was allowing your horse to trample a hound. *Baily's* reported how some 'delinquents' tried to defend themselves:

Baronet to Cad: 'Dear, dear me, you have killed my hound'.
Cad: 'Don't be the least alarmed, Sir. I have been trying for years to kill a hound and have never yet succeeded.'

And…

'Thrusting rider' explaining to His Lordship why he has crashed into an elderly hound as the creature was splayed arthritically half way across a fence: 'I can assure you, my Lord, the old hound could never have got into the next field but for the assistance I gave him'.

DO YOU KNOW THE TYPE?

'As no well-regulated family is complete without a black sheep, so no hunt is complete without a swell…Here he comes now, fresh from his valet, who is likewise fresh from the tailor. You feel like betting ten to one the clothes he wears are not paid for. But no matter. He had to do it. In fact, it was the sight of the latest hunting fashion-plate that decided him to take up hunting. His appearance gives a deal of harmless amusement to the other members. He has choked himself with a stock, and wears a corset, or looks as if he did, in his wasp-waisted hunting-coat. He wears number seven patent-leather boots on a number eight foot. What an unhappy, uncomfortable person he looks !

How can he be otherwise with his horse a long-legged, light-waisted, three-cornered animal of the weedy thoroughbred order? Altogether he resembles a gaudy rider in the show-ring. After a good pull or two of jumping-powder from a gold-mounted flask, he is quite fit to make a spectacle of himself. He generally gets a damning from the Master, either mentally or orally, for riding too near his hounds, and seems utterly regardless of any rule of hunting.'

From Cross Country With Horse And Hound, *by Frank Sherman Peer, 1902. Peer was an American, whose book was the first to be published in America devoted entirely to foxhunting the English way. Peer had an excellent grasp of the sport thanks to endless English hunting acquaintances. In common with hunting journalists of his era, Peer loved mixing with nobs. He liberally dropped names such as Lonsdale and Rothschild. He wrote of his admiration for the aristocracy: 'In the hunting field in England everyone seems to meet on a level. An English gentleman holds his standing so securely that he can speak with any one of his acquaintance without ever feeling that he has lowered himself in doing so. Altogether an English gentleman is the most gentlemanly gentleman in the world (except to strangers)'.*

Peer's book was dedicated to the Meadow Brook Hounds, a posh hunt in Long Island, New York, which faded away in the 1940s as development swallowed up their country. Some Meadow Brook facts:

• The Meadow Brook was the world's first hunt to be featured in a documentary, in 1899.

• The most famous subscriber to the Meadow Brook was President Theodore Roosevelt, who wrote of foxhunting, 'The fox is hunted (in Long Island) merely because there is no larger game to follow. As long as wolves, deer or antelope remain in the land no one would think of following the fox.'

• Most Meadow Brook subscribers preferred the convenience of drag hunting. A local newspaper reported, 'At least half of the Meadow Brook's members are men of business, who go daily to New York. They get home by an afternoon train, and by dint of hurrying, gain two or three hours from the working-day, which they can spend on a horse's back. When they go to the meet, at three o'clock or thereabouts, there is not time for an indefinite search after a fox, even if the country were favourable to such a quest. The Meadow Brook men want a sure run whenever they go out…and they want it to end with certainty in time for dinner'.

WAGGING THE BRUSH

'WITH THE FOX, an explosive snarl or spit dignifies displeasure, while pleasure, as in greeting another fox, may be shown by laying back the ears, grinning widely and wagging the brush. Under the pressure of breeding season emotions the vixen often gives vent to a weird screech or scream; she also utters some weird sounds when calling her cubs. The dog-fox has a barking cry chiefly heard at mating time in the early part of the New Year. He does not bark continuously like a dog, but utters a short, gruff sound three or four times and then pauses, as if to listen for a reply, before repeating it. Thus a fox will serenade his lady love for some time. It is often stated that the vixen does not and cannot bark, but I would not like to be too positive on this point; certainly the screech is her more usual cry, and equally certain the dog-fox is the songster of the firm. To compare his call with the song of a bird may seem odd, but I believe it to be akin in function, an advertisement of his whereabouts, a warning-off notice to other males, and an invitation to the female.'

From In Praise of Hunting *by 1960s radio naturalist and Shropshire MFH Frances Pitt, Hollis & Carter, 1960*

AS IF IT COULD POSSIBLY MATTER

An anti-motor car rant by Lady Augusta Fane in her
1926 memoir *Chit-Chat:*

'MOTOR CARS HAVE SPOILT HUNTING. They enable a crowd of strangers to hunt where they do not live, and where they consequently spend no money and do no good to the farmers. Tarmac roads are most dangerous for horses, as they cannot get a foothold on a wet day, and there have been many serious accidents from horses slipping and falling on their riders. Much good fellowship has been lost now that hacking to covert has ended. The country roads are no longer quiet and peaceful, and it is hard to find any place that is free of noise and the smell of petrol. I often long for the scent of fresh hay in a stable and the soft whinnying of one's favourite hunter for the expected carrot; instead I am led into a stuffy garage with the chauffeur running the engines. This is a mechanical age, the youngest children know the name of every car and talk learnedly of the difference between a Rolls and Buick, and the moment anybody arrives on a visit he or she recounts excitedly how many hundred miles they have done in a couple of hours! As if it could possibly matter or be of the slightest interest.'

From Chit-Chat *by Lady Augusta Fane, Thornton, Butterworth, Ltd*

> • When first invented, the motor car caused havoc in the hunting field. Some Masters banned these hideous beasts on the grounds that petrol fumes ruined scent. Subscribers were requested to park their lorries well away from the meet and hack the last mile or two. Meanwhile, it became fashionable for supporters to 'hunt from the chassis'. *Baily's Hunting Directory* warned, 'Motor cars are an ever increasing source of trouble'.

Not all Masters hated the car. The pride and joy of Sir Hercules Langrishe, Master of the Kilkenny, was a Panhard-Levassor one of the earliest petrol vehicles – 2-cylinder sidevalve, 673 cc producing 7 bhp, max 40 mph. A slow beast, but terrifying to the unitiated horse.

In 1904 Sir Hercules contributed an essay on motoring to a 1904 compendium titled *Motors and Motor-Driving*: 'I hunt my own hounds four days a week, my distances are very long indeed, and I found in former seasons that after a hard week I had had more than enough of it. In the summer of 1902 I bought the Panhard and told my supporters that I intended using it exclusively to convey me to the meets during the coming season. Their consternation was extreme. Some were amused, some horrified at the idea, but I carried out my intention to the very letter, not employing any other means of conveyance to take me to any meet above two miles from my own hall door. All the hunters got used to the motor almost at once, and now it is no uncommon thing to see five or six cars at a meet. Of course if one observes a farmer on a young horse, or a second horseman leading another, one naturally pulls up if the creatures are the least frightened, and allows them to trot on to a gate but this does not often occur'.

Sir Hercules summed up the motoring revolution: 'To forbid a gentleman to drive to a meet in his automobile for no other reason than 'because he might frighten the horses,' really does seem to me to be simply childish. We surely are lot such a lot of old women as to be afraid that we shall fall if that 'horrid noisy thing ' comes near us. The anti-motorist may love the horse, I love him too, but on hunting days I do not wish to see my horse till I arrive at the meet'.

> • Leicestershire landowner Sir Harold Nutting, Master of the Quorn 1932–40, had little time for the motor car. If someone rang him before a meet asking where they should leave their vehicle, he would reply, 'In your garage, I hope', and ring off.

UNEMPLOYED ON BICYCLES

MINOR ARISTOCRAT LORD STALBRIDGE, Master of the Fernie in the 1920s, viewed the general public as a frightful nuisance. He complained that uninvited onlookers were cluttering up his meets, the worst offenders being 'the unemployed on bicycles and ladies in limousines'. Hunting was for those who rode to hounds and was not to be shared.

Having inherited the Motcombe Park estate, near Port Regis, Wiltshire, Hughie, 2nd Baron Stalbridge, son of a prominent Liberal politician, sold part of it in the early 1920s in order to finance his new passion for hunting in Leicestershire. He bought his way into Mastership of the Fernie by paying for new kennels at Bowden. And when he tired of life in Leicestershire he returned to Wiltshire where he built yet another new kennels complex, this time for the South and West Wilts. He is possibly the only Master to have paid for two sets of brand new kennels for two different hunts.

BONES ONLY BENT

A is Ambition which leads you to buy
A qualified hunter, the picture of pride,
Of whom it is said, 'He takes off in his stride',
This means he jumps you off with hounds in full cry.

F is the Fence made of stout posts and rails
Five feet! You 'sailed over it riding the grey'.
But do not dine out on it often, I pray,
For at each repetition the interest pales.

G is the Gathering Gloom of Her Grace,
The Great One, invited to open our Ball,
When she heard that the Master had had a bad fall
And the Honorable Whip is to fill in his place.

K is the Kennels where foxhounds are kept,
A visit to these is a part of the Game;
'Tis a wise MFH knows each couple by name,
But when they know him they say strong men have wept.

N is the Nag, 'Nervy Nat' who was lent
For your use by a friend when your own horse broke down,
And the News, that was sent to your dear ones in Town,
'Some bones have been broken and some are just bent'.

O is the Opportune Offer you made
To carry a flask in case of a spill;
Then you learn that it's equally good for a chill
And most of the field of a chill are afraid.

P is for 'Pink' to its pomp we aspire
When riding in 'mufti'; but how do we feel
When bound for the Meet, quite the modern John Peel,
If village boys shout, 'Oh, I say, where's the fire?'

From The ABC Of Drag Hunting, *by American poet*
Grace Clarke Newton, 1917

UNDERBRED AND OBNOXIOUS

FREDERICK DELME RADCLIFFE, Master of the Hertfordshire Hunt 1835-9, argued that good breeding was essential for hounds, horses and men. 'In ninety-nine cases out of a hundred, where the harmony of any society is disturbed by an obnoxious individual, then he is usually a low underbred fellow; one in short, who never could have had a grandfather.' Delme Radcliffe was author of a much-read book titled *The Noble Science Of Foxhunting.*

HOSSES LIKE IT

A STORY DID THE ROUNDS IN VICTORIAN ENGLAND concerning an elderly huntsman who invited a countess to visit his kennels.

'Certainly not!' answered the haughty lady. 'I dislike everything about hunting. It is so cruel.'

'Cruel?' replied the old man in astonishment. 'Why, my lady, it can't possibly be cruel, for…'. And he held up three fingers…

'We all knows that the gentlemen like it,

'And we all knows that the hosses like it,

'And we all knows that the hounds like it,

'And,' after a pause he added, 'None of us can know for certain that the foxes don't like it'.

FOXES PLENTY

'To hounds stout, and horses healthy,
Earths well stopp'd and foxes plenty'.

Old hunting toast, said to have originated in Oxfordshire.

BAD BET

A terrifying lady called Betty Berners was MFH with the Old Berkshire during the 1960s. Wife of Geoffrey, Lord Berners whose family owned a large chunk of property in London's West End, Betty had strong views on what constituted a gentleman. One day, to her horror, the Old Berks was joined by a hunting novice in the form of a croupier from Aspinalls. Soon after setting off the man fell off his horse in a gateway in front of the entire field. Betty was unfazed. She spurred her horse passed the recumbent figure face down in the mud, announcing to all, 'Leave him! Leave him! I think he's dead'.

MEAT RATION

THE ECCENTRICITY of the foxhunter is illustrated by Major-General Tom Bridges who commanded the 19th Division at Flanders in 1917. Bridges had a pet lion, named Poilu, which was envied by the men because of the huge size of his meat ration. Bridges had acquired Poilu as a cub in Paris in spring 1916. The animal accompanied the General in his staff car and was apparently friendly.

During the Battle of Flanders, Bridges was badly wounded and doctors wanted to take his leg off. The general was reluctant to let them do this because it meant he would never be able to hunt again. But the doctors insisted.

'All right,' Bridges said. 'You can take it off, but only on condition that you feed it to my lion.'

It is not known whether Poilu received his extra ration. Soon afterwards the animal was repatriated to a private zoo in England where he lived to the age of nineteen. Bridges became Governor of Australia during the 1920s. He died in 1939.

OH TO BE BORN A HOUND

JOHN BYNG, a visitor to the Duke of Bedford's new hunt kennels at Woburn in 1794, was horrified to see that they were far superior to the servants' quarters. The kennels had a special kitchen with boilers and separate apartments for the bitches during pregnancy. Everything was beautifully clean. The staff rooms next door, noted Byng, were 'miserable hovels erected for the sons of Adam who…regret they are not born foxhounds'.

BOOZY RANT

JOHN PEEL, most famous huntsman of them all, was a farmer from Cumberland who hunted his own pack of hounds over today's Blencathra country from 1798 to his death in 1854. Like many obsessive foxhunters he spent most of his money on his sport. His fondness for booze didn't help either. After a particularly good day on the fells he would go on a forty-eight-hour bender.

Dressed in his 'coat so grey' – made of hairy Cumberland wool known as hoddengray – Peel hunted mostly on foot. The song about him, *D'ye Ken John Peel?*, was written by his friend John Woodcock Graves, who based it on a Scottish 'rant' called Bonnie Annie. Despite boosting Peel's public image with his words, Graves privately despaired of his friend's extravagance and his hunting mania: 'Business of any shape was utterly neglected…indeed this neglect extended to paternal duties of his family. I believe he would not have left the drag of a fox on the impending death of a child or any other earthly event.'

Peel died from a fall in the hunting field on 13 November 1854. Around 3,000 people attended his funeral. His wife Lettice and family were left destitute, kept only by gifts from friends. His sons were snapped up as servants by the local gentry who were keen to claim a link with their famous father.

• D'ye Ken John Peel was sung by the soldiers of the 34th and 35th of Foot at the Relief of Lucknow in 1857. The following year the song became a hit in London drawing rooms after being rearranged by composer William Metcalfe, lay clerk of Carlisle Cathedral. Sheet copies were sold across the British Empire.

• In 1977 John Peel's family grave was desecrated by hunt saboteurs.

• John Peel's name was taken by the Radio One DJ, born John Ravenscroft, while he was starting out in radio during the 1960s. The moniker was suggested by a Radio London secretary who enjoyed hunting. Won't find many of those at the BBC these days.

A VERY GOOD NOSE

CAPTAIN PATRICK CARNEGY, early nineteenth century Master of the Forfarshire Hounds, had blown hounds out of covert after drawing a blank when a member of the field rode up and said, 'There's a fox left in there'.

'I think not, and nor do my hounds,' Carnegy said.

'But I can smell him,' said the member of the field.

'Can you indeed, sir? In which case you must have a very good nose. Come round to kennels tomorrow and we'll put you to our best bitch.'

GETTING THE HORN

'Nothing sounds worse in the hunting field than discordant horn music, and nothing looks worse than an amateur blowing himself black in the face, and succeeding only in producing horrible noises, as of someone in his death agony.'

Richard Clapham, Foxes, Foxhounds and Foxhunting *1922*.

Clapham was a naturalist and foxhunter from the Lake District. He pointed out that in the middle-ages there were many different sounds played on the hunting horn. But modern hunting was an altogether duller affair. 'Sometimes you hear nothing but a single monotonous note blown all day, or a few calls seldom repeated. Hunting in the open there is of course but little real need for a variety of horn music, such as our French friends use in their woodland hunting. Of modern calls we have a single note when hounds are off to draw, and the 'gone away' when a fox breaks covert. Then on a scent the huntsman may perhaps 'double the horn,' and when hounds are eating their fox he sounds the 'rattle'. At the end of the day he may blow a long note or several short ones followed by a long one, to warn the field that hounds are going home.'

BERMUDA BAGS

THE BRITISH tried hunting in Bermuda in the early 1870s but the sport never took off. The 1st Battalion, 20th Regiment established the Bermuda Hunt Club and imported a pack of hounds and several crates of English foxes in order to hunt on ground outside St George's. But the supply of foxes ran out after a year.

The club lowered its sights and continued to operate as a 'paper' hunt. An ex-pat called Jane Eames, writing from Bermuda in 1875, described a St Patrick's day meet:

'As there are no foxes or deer to hunt on these islands, this club gets up, now and then, a mock hunt. Two horsemen in huntsman array go ahead, scattering pieces of paper in their wake, and the remainder of the hunting party, on horseback, of course, go wherever these scraps of paper dictate.

'It was an animated scene, I can assure you, the spectators arriving in carriages, while various members of the hunting party galloped about on their fiery steeds, impatient for the chase. Away they all went, at a given signal, leaping fences and stone walls, and darting across the country, while we followed in our carriages so as to meet them at a given spot on their return; and then it was such a pretty sight to see them come galloping along the brow of a hill, leaping over walls, fences, ditches, and every other obstruction in their headlong career. This was more like an English hunt than anything we have ever seen out of dear old England, and we enjoyed it immensely.'

BAD REGIME

'If a MFH cannot keep order without bad language and much scolding, he is scarcely the right man in the right place, and will only be tolerated if the sport shown under his regime is of an exceptionally high order.'

From A Hunting Catechism, *by Colonel Richard Meysey-Thompson, 1907*

A TOPPING GALLOP

THE SHANGHAI PAPER HUNT, founded in the 1860s, featured a human 'fox' dressed in a red cowl – à la Red Riding Hood – laying a paper trail. The pack consisted of hounds imported from Scotland, but the actual chase was little more than a glorified point to point.

The Paper Hunt was scorned by old China hands such as Maurice Springfield, founder of the Shanghai Hounds before the First World War. The Shanghai was a drag pack that was sometimes allowed to hunt live quarry.

Springfield experimented with all manner of scents. 'Aniseed oil gave the poorest results. The hair combings off a Siberian stag, a tricky business in the rutting season, was quite good, but far and away the best for music and drive was Himalayan bear urine mixed with porcupine droppings (provided by Shanghai Zoo.) The porcupine itself was added after a terrific hunt after one in hill country about 100 miles from Shanghai. Hounds simply revelled in this scent which lay well even in a drought.'

Springfield remembered an evening after a good drag hunt when he bumped into a Japanese exchange broker in the bar at the Shanghai Race Club. 'I told him what a topping gallop we had had and asked why he had not been out. "Ah! my friend", he said, "I marry off my eldest daughter today. I give her good advice. I say to her ride with Mr. Springfield's hounds – then you will not have so many babies as your mother." The mother, poor woman, was said to have an odd existence. If her husband won a race he would give her yet another pearl for her necklace. If his pony lost he thrashed her with his riding whip.'

From Hunting Opium and Other Scents, *by Maurice Springfield, Norfolk and Suffolk Publicity, 1966*

GO FOR THE BEST

'A bad horse cannot get over the country at all, and a second class one will only spoil your pleasure and ruin your nerve.'

Captain Edward Pennell Elmhirst, The Field's *late nineteenth century hunting correspondent better known as 'Brooksby'*

IRISH LUCK

Luckiest MFH was a young man called John Ryan who in the years before the First World War ran his family's Scarteen Hunt with its famous Black and Tan hounds on the Limerick-Tipperary border. When war broke out Ryan was sent to the front with the 16th Lancers. During an enemy barrage he and several of his soldiers were blown up and buried by heavy shellfire. He was listed as killed.

Unknown to the British, the Germans found Ryan alive and sent him to a prisoner of war camp. There he was spotted by a German officer who by amazing coincidence had hunted with the Scarteen in peacetime. The German arranged special privileges for Ryan and managed to get word back to Ireland that the lad was safe.

That week, as the mail train pulled into small stations throughout the west of Ireland the engineer would cry out, 'The Master's alive! The Master's alive!' Bonfires were lit in Ryan's home village of Emly, and the committee collecting money for the memorial decided that rather than refunding the subscriptions, it would simplify matters if the funds were spent on whisky. The booze-up lasted nine days.

AND THEY SAY HUNTING IS FUN

You needed a death wish to hunt in nineteenth century Leicestershire. One day in the winter of 1885 the Quorn had a remarkably good run culminating in one of the most terrifying leaps ever attempted – a brook that had been dug out the day before and now spanned 22 feet bank to bank. The hounds piled into the water and struggled to the other side. There was no time for the lead horses to stop. Of the bunch that took the jump only three landed on the far side. Everyone else fell. Two horses broke their backs. The water was strewn with bruised riders. The fox was eventually killed a few fields further on. Afterwards the brook was railed off and a warning sign erected with the words: 'Dead Man's Hole'.

HOW YOUR PACK CAN FORECAST THE WEATHER

'Sign, too, of rain; his outstretched feet the hound
Extends, and curves his belly to the ground.'

From Phaenomena by Greek didactic poet Aratus (c. 315–240 BC) whose
work included numerous ways of predicting the weather. (Shooting men
may be interested to know that Aratus says if spaniels sleep more than usual
it foretells wet weather. Likewise it will rain if dogs eat grass.)

SHOCKING BAD HUNTER

'THERE ARE A FEW MEN IN EVERY LARGE HUNT, and an odd one
in every small hunt, who can go in front on any and every sort of horse, and
can keep them there as long as condition of their horses will allow of it. Not
only are such men fine horsemen, but they are gifted with some indescribable
knack of getting along. They have falls, of course, but no more than their
neighbours when their style of riding is taken into consideration, and what
they really excel in is that they are able to make horses gallop and jump in a
way which is an impossibility to other men. It is not the honest, willing horse
that they are seen to so much advantage on, but the raw, ignorant horse, or
very often the animal which is in ordinary hands a shocking bad hunter'.

From The Complete Foxhunter, *by Charles Richardson, 1908. Richardson was
hunting editor of* The Field

HUNTING IS GOOD FOR YOUR HEALTH

'Allah does not count to a man the years spent in the chase.'

Arab epigram

HOW TO CHEAT AT THE PUPPY SHOW

'During the summer it is usual to hold what is known as the "puppy show". This is a function that arouses the greatest interest in hounds and their pedigrees amongst the members of the hunt. But for the show it would be hard to discover that any interest at all was ever taken in such trifling matters. Should the Master elect to avoid the anxiety and disappointment of hound breeding, he may easily do so without in the least affecting this popular annual gathering. A sharp huntsman will rise to the occasion, and will draft from the pack a suitable number of the freshest and best-looking hounds he can find. These will represent the "young entry"of the year. The Master will see that a neighbouring MFH or two are invited to judge, and that a printed list of hound names, arranged so as to appear in litters, with the respective sire and dam, are distributed amongst the guests. If this is done properly and with ordinary care, a very creditable show may be held. Of course should one of the judges discover the ruse the Master would be in a very awkward dilemma, but this calamity is highly unlikely to occur. If it did, a rapid adjournment to the luncheon tent is the wisest move. There, under the beneficent influence of an unknown vintage, all will be forgotten and forgiven. If the huntsman has discharged his task of selection properly, the judges will most likely say that the entry is one of the best and strongest they have ever seen. The Hunt Committee will be much gratified to think that the destinies of their hunt are confided to the care of such an excellent Master.'

C. W. Bell, author of the humorous 1899 book Foxhunting: A Treatise, *by 'The Rt. Hon. The Earl of Kilreynard'*

FORBIDDINGLY KEEN

THE MOST FAMOUS RUN IN THE HISTORY OF HUNTING is the Quorn's Billesdon Coplow Run of 24 February 1800. The Master in charge of this glorious morning was the hunt's founder Hugo Meynell, in his last year of the mastership.

The run commenced with the second find of the morning when 200 horses started away with hounds after a fox roused in Billesdon Coplow covert, a wooded knoll 625 feet above east Leicestershire.

The fox took the hunt past Tilton Wood, across the River Soar below Whitestone, past Galby, Norton, Great and Little Stretton, by Old Stretton Hall, and on to Wigston and Ayleston, up to Enderby Gorse, where nearly all the field gave up. Only four horseman, including the huntsman Jack Raven, were in at the kill.

The distance was twenty-eight miles run in two hours, fifteen minutes, an average speed of twelve mph. Horses and hounds were exhausted. In those days the country would have been undrained and a twenty-eight mile gallop over heavy ground would have put a huge strain on the animals. On the plus side there would have been few fences to jump. The fields were mostly covered with rough grass, and the only big obstacles were brooks with not a single fence between the castles of Nottingham and Belvoir.

• One of the horses in the Billesdon Coplow was a mare called The Widow, owned by a Captain White who had been one of the foremost riders during the run. The horse was due to be sold the following the week at Melton Mowbray Old Club auctions with an estimate of £400. Such was the Widow's fame following the run that it fetched £600. Captain White was a fearless foxhunter. He lived in digs at a house in Melton known as Claret Lodge because of the vast amount of wine consumed there. Legend has it that following the Billesdon Coplow, White was so exhausted that when he got home he broke with custom, ignored the booze and instead settled down for a plain mutton chop and a cup of tea. 'Altogether an extraordinary day for him', remarked a friend.

• Nearly one hundred years after the Billesdon Coplow, on 14 December 1894, the Quorn witnessed another remarkable run known as the Barkby Holt. The Quorn's bitch pack followed a fox over twenty-seven miles for two hours and five minutes until he went to ground in a rabbit hole. What was remarkable about the Barkby Holt Run was that the Master, Lord Lonsdale, and all the hunt servants were at the finish, having kept up with hounds for the entire distance.

• Other great runs include:

MR. DELME RADCLIFFE'S WENDOVER RUN. 17 March 1837. Found at 2.30 pm. 2 hours 35 minutes. Fox lost as dusk. 18 miles point to point; hounds ran 26 miles. Next morning fox found dead in rick yard, possibly from exhaustion.

THE OLD FINDON (SURREY). 9 February 1849. Fox run for 45 miles in 4 hours, 50 minutes. Last 22 miles nearly straight. Fox killed in Dorking Glory.

WATERLOO RUN (THE PYTCHLEY), 2 February 1866. Found in Waterloo Gorse 2.05 pm. 18 miles in one hour fifty minutes without a check, crossing only three ploughed fields. The night of the run Pytchley MFH Jack Anstruther Thomson was cheered at the hunt ball at Market Harborough. Anstruther Thomson spent most of his family money on hunting. He was a huge, extrovert man – 6 ft 2 ins, 16 stone – who preferred to crash through hedges rather than jump them. Someone described him as 'a sight to watch rather than a tempting example to follow'. Note: it must be said that although the Waterloo was 'bigged up' by the Pytchley, one horseman carped later that it was more like a 'journey' rather than a proper run. 'Hounds were continually changing foxes and were never near catching one of them.'

THE RADBURNE RUN (MEYNELL), 3 February 1868. Fast but erratic run, 3 hours 37 minutes. 36 miles. Fox retired exhausted with hounds nowhere to be seen. Fox knocked on the head by a farmer.

THE DUKE OF BEAUFORT'S GREAT RUN, 22 February 1871. Found Gretenham Great Wood. 3 hours 26 minutes. 14 miles point to point. 28 miles as hounds ran.

MR CHAWORTH MUSTERS' HARLEQUIN RUN. Ash Wednesday, 16 February 1872. Arguably the second greatest run in the history of foxhunting. Found in Harlequin Gorse. 3 hours 26 minutes. Over 35 miles. 15 and a half couple out of 17 and a half couple of hounds in at the kill. Yes, fox actually caught. Almost as remarkable was the poem written to commemorate the run by Henry Smith, son of one of the riders and no more than twelve-years-old:

Come, pull off your boots, 'tis no time for a nap;
Let us measure the run on the Ordnance Map;
Much fun have we seen since the frost, but this last day
Proves the joke that Ash Wednesday's a regular 'fast day'.

Experience endorses the dogma,
That good hounds will beat good horses;
Strangers from Quorn or Pytchley, if you doubt,
Bring down your gee gees, and let's see them out;
Let's see them out on such like day, and you
Will all admit my theory is true:
For time, and points, and country, all attest
The finest run recorded in the west.

MR. ROLLESTON'S LOWDHAM RUN, 9 February 1881. Ran 16 miles, gave up at dusk. Very fast all the way, time not recorded.

THE SYDMONTON RUN (THE CRAVEN). 2 January 1899. 10 miles point to point, hounds ran 20 miles. First 10 miles so fast nobody could get near hounds.

• It is generally considered that the very long runs were petering out by the end of the twentieth century thanks to the increasing hindrance of wire. However, the twentieth century saw some impressive hunts including the Barkby Holt (Quorn, 27 March 1903,); the Horninghold (Mr Fernie's, 25 February 1911, 30 miles, three and a half hours, only four of original field in at the kill); the Clawson Thorns (Belvoir, 9 January 1926, 29 miles of country covered, four and a half hours, horsemen included Prince of Wales, Duke of York, Prince Henry.) Former *Horse & Hound* editor Michael Clayton recalls in his 2004 book *Endangered Species* a splendid run that took place with the Cottesmore in February 2004. 'This was a fine hunt with a point of over nine miles, and a run of about fifteen – statistics worthy of hunts in the "golden age" of foxhunting.'

STOLID AND GRUMPY RIDERS

SCOUTS FOUNDER LORD BADEN-POWELL was a keen foxhunter who became Master of the Cape Foxhounds in South Africa in the years before the Boer War.

'We had some very keen if weird-looking followers of the hunt before that wretched war', he wrote, referring to the scruffy Dutchmen who would turn up at meets 'mounted on their wiry unkempt little horses, their rusty bits and stirrups being as unlike the turn-out of the English hunting-field as are the riders' corduroy trousers, hobnailed boots, and wide flapping hats'.

But the Boer horsemen could equal England's finest. 'The riders, stolid and grumpy as is their demeanour, will rouse up like schoolboys and go with the keenest when once there is fox afoot…' But Baden-Powell added mournfully, 'Had that bond of sportsmanship been allowed to continue which brought Boer and Briton together in the hunting field, there would today have been a close feeling of friendship, if not a fusion of the two races in those parts'.

To Baden-Powell, hunting was everything that was important to England. He wrote in his book *Sport in War*: 'Fox-hunting, when you come to think of it, is really a very wonderful institution. Although it has come to be quite an artificial sport in a wholly civilised country it still keeps going in every part of England in spite of the (Boer) war, in spite of the decline in horse-breeding, and in spite of heavy taxes and heavier costs. It is one of the few old institutions left which still keeps us in touch to-day with the traditions and spirit of the former Old England'.

> • The Cape Hunt, founded 1822, is the oldest of the new world hunts. The first Cape Hunt foxhounds came from the Beaufort and were imported into South Africa by the Cape Governor, Lord Charles Somerset. It is now a drag hunt.

FOPS THAT MAKE A BUSINESS OF SPORT

Eighteenth century foxhunters were often the butt of jokes, as shown in this satirical discourse between love rivals Mr Wildish and Lord Bellamy in Thomas Shadwell's 1689 comedy *Bury Fair*.

Mr Wildish: 'But what can be the diversion of a country life? A man must be woken at 3 o'clock in the morning by the cracked voice of huntsmen, with damned bugle horns, and the confounded yelps of curs; and for want of friendship with men divert themselves with their enmity to beasts; and hunt as if the devil were in 'em, til at dark night they are scarce able to dismount their horses.'

Lord Bellamy: 'They are fops, Ned, that make a business of sport. I hunt with my harriers half a dozen heats in a morning for health and an appetite; and at dinner time, let 'em be in never such full cry, I knock off.'

Mr Wildish: 'There is some reason in that; but your true country squire lives in boots all the winter, never talks of anything but sports, as he calls 'em, and if an ill day comes, saunters about his house, lolls on couches, sighs and groans as if he were a prisoner in the Fleet; and the best thing he can find to do is to smoke and drink and play at backgammon with the parson.'

Lord Bellamy: 'These are the strictest order of hunters, such as keep journals of everyday's hunting and write long letters of fox chases from one end of England to the other.'

CLEANSING DOSE

'It might do his cause no harm if the foxhunter were to point out…that comparatively few of the semi-intoxicated bright young things whose portraits appear taken at hunt balls in the society press are hunting people; rather they are the social riff-raff of the towns, whose minds and bodies could well do with a cleansing dose of foxhunting.'

David Brock, MFH, 1939

A DIET OF BOOTS

'...Hound puppies. I was reminded of them today, as I passed near the stables on my way out to shoot, and there I saw a hound puppy on a lawn quietly eating a boot. Hound puppies are sent out in pairs to houses throughout the county in the summer and are brought up on a diet of boots and rags, varied by an occasional hat, and find their own sport, chasing whatever will run in coverts near to the house....Just when one is getting to know them rather well, they are called for and taken away from their life of indiscipline, to be members of a pack, and to learn no more to look at a rabbit than a soldier would play on parade with some toy of his infancy.'

From My Ireland, *by Lord Dunsany, 1922*

TABLE MATS

'My dining room curtains and my place mats are covered with hunting scenes, something which puzzles those visitors who are aware of my strong anti-hunting views, but I explain that I consider the hunt a colourful feature of Olde England and that in Olde England it firmly belongs. A meet may be a splendid and traditional sight but I find no place for it in a modern, humane society.'

Anne Widdecombe, ex-MP

SWEEP AFTER BRUSH

Much to the surprise of the gentlemen of the Grafton Hunt during the mid-nineteenth century, they were joined by a foxhunting chimney sweep from Stony Stratford named Adam Sherwood. Sherwood cleaned the chimneys of the local country houses and was quite well to do. The Grafton members accepted him as one of their own because he was good company. On hunting days Sherwood wore a quaint 'chimney pot' top hat, of which, according to a fellow Graftonite, 'the altitude had been considerably lowered by repeated bangs upon the top'.

• Sherwood was famous for his double hip flask which consisted of two glass bottles welded together. One dispensed brandy and the other gin, depending on his mood.

LIKE THE VERY DEVIL

THE VICTORIAN HUNTING JOURNALIST SURTEES had a thing about women out hunting: 'A man does not like riding before them, or leaving them in the lurch; and even if they do go along the whole field is kept in alarm lest an accident happen'. But even Surtees admitted: 'When women do ride, they generally ride like the very devil'.

GOOD HUNTING

'And now gentlemen, I wish you all "Good Hunting"'. Conclusion of Field Marshal Bernard Montgomery's speech to senior officers before the Battle of El Alamein, 1942.

This is a curious reference to the noble science because Monty was not known as a hunting man. However, his opposite American number, General George Patton, loved the chase. One of the richest officers in the U.S. Army, Patton always arrived at a new posting with a hunter or two in tow.

RICH

You had to be mighty rich to hunt, rest and play with the Pytchley Hunt Club of the eighteenth century. Limited to forty members of the sporting aristocracy and gentry, it was nicknamed 'The Pelican' because of the size of its bills. Members were expected to spend up to £5000 per annum (in the region of half a million pounds today) for dining, gambling, horse-dealing and general roistering. Members had an after-dinner custom of placing a half crown in one of their wine goblets. The unfortunate member who found the coin after draining his glass had to put up all his horses for sale whether he liked it or not.

The club disbanded in 1816. An observer remarked, 'Many of the original members had died off, got married or turned over a new leaf'.

• England's oldest surviving hunt club is the Tarporley Hunt Club in Cheshire. Many of the forty members (uniform: scarlet coat with green collar) are keen hunting people; the Prince of Wales is a patron. These days the Tarporley is primarily a dining club. It still meets in the Hunt Room in its original HQ, a pub called the Swan in the Cheshire village of Tarporley. Although the Swan was sold some years ago, the club have retained a 999-year lease on their room, which is adorned with memorabilia and paintings.

• The oldest surviving hunt club in the British Isles is the Down Hunt Club, based at Downpatrick, County Antrim. The Down Hunt toasts include the traditional 'to hunting' and the reassuringly Celtic 'to any other excuse for another glass'.

SIR GILBERT, ON MAYNELL.

SKINT

By 1880 the Pytchley Hunt was in bad financial trouble. Despite attracting huge fields the hunt was always short of cash thanks to the paucity of its subscribers. The Master, Herbert Langham was permanently skint, and the last straw was the day when the whip arrived at the meet on a bicycle and had to explain that the bailiffs wouldn't let the hunt horses out of the stables. In 1890 the hunt was rescued by Lord Spencer who contributed substantial funds to keep it afloat.

THE INWARDLY ASHAMED TAKING REVENGE

'THE (HUNTING) BAN has patently become a form of transference activity for Labour. Several commentators, notably in the *Guardian*, and even one or two Labour MPs, have asked why on earth Parliament has wasted so much time on this question when there are many more important matters to tackle, but here is the answer. 'Si vendicano gli uomini delle leggiere offese; delli gravi non possono': hunting is a fine example of Machiavelli's saying that men take revenge for small offences, unable to avenge the larger ones. Socialism is dead, along with most of what those (Labour) MPs once believed in, and the knowledge of that has morally corroded them. They are inwardly ashamed of themselves, and they search for one token issue to make themselves feel good. The Bill assuages MPs' self-hatred and sense of their own betrayal, so that a former radical like Peter Hain, now a Cabinet minister working with servile loyalty for a government he would once have hated, insists on forcing through the Hunting Bill'.

Geoffrey Wheatcroft, The Spectator, *November 2004*

INVALUABLE HINT

'To those foxhunters who do not care to risk the danger of riding over fences, and yet do not wish to expose themselves to the ridicule of their friends, the author will give an invaluable hint. Let the rider be careful to exhibit the greatest anxiety to get a good start, to show that he really means business. Then, when he hears the ' forward away,' he must cram down his hat as far over his head as it will go, at the same time vigorously applying the spur to his horse (whose tail should now revolve rapidly), and gallop away as fast as he can. This conveys a fine impression to all who see it. When the inevitable happens, and the sportsman finds himself in a field from which there is no exit but the gate by which he entered, he must assume a look of great determination. Catching hold of his horse tightly by the head, he should drive him at the thickest place in the fence. On arriving within taking off distance, the hold upon the horse should be suddenly relaxed. This will, in nine cases out of ten, cause the animal to refuse. These tactics may be repeated until the rest of the field have disappeared, when the sportsman can return to the road. Should anyone happen to be present, it is as well to flog the horse soundly, and denounce him as being a stubborn brute that has again lost the rider a real good thing.'

From Foxhunting: A Treatise (1899), *by 'The Rt. Hon. The Earl of Kilreynard' aka humorist and foxhunter C. W. Bell*

FARMER'S SON FOXES HUNTERS

IN 1878 THE HIGH COURT HEARD an extraordinary case in which two members of the Taunton Vale, Mr Paul and Mr Summerhayes appealed against their conviction for attacking a farmer's son who attempted to prevent them from entering one of his father's fields in pursuit of a fox. The foxhunters claimed that it was the farmer's son who should have been in the dock for attacking them. Demonstrating considerable chutzpah, the pair's barrister argued that foxhunting was such an important sport that it could be carried out over someone's land without permission.

To nobody's surprise, the judge, Lord Coleridge, ruled that no such right existed even if the hunting fraternity liked to think it did. 'The sport of foxhunting must be carried on in subordination to the ordinary rights of property', the judge said. 'Questions such as the present fortunately do not often arise, because those who pursue the sport of foxhunting do so in a reasonable spirit'.

TRUE WORDS

'A fox is a good friend to lazy gamekeepers ; any harm done by any other vermin is always put down to the fox'.

From A Hunting Catechism *by Colonel Richard Meysey-Thompson, 1907*

IDLE DOG

WORST JOB EVER IN FOXHUNTING was that of huntsman to John Elwes, who despite having inherited a large south London brewing fortune, was described as eighteenth century England's greatest miser.

The story has it that during the season Elwes forced his wretched servant to get up at four every morning, milk the house cows, prepare breakfast for his master and any guests, then put on a green coat, saddle the horses, get out the hounds, and prepare everything for a day's hunting. At the end of the day he would rub down the horses, go inside to prepare dinner for the Master, and then return to the stables, milk the cows, rub down the horses and feed the hounds before being allowed to go to bed.

During this hell of a day, Elwes would refer to his pathetic minion as 'an idle dog'. Elwes died in 1789 alone in an empty London house (he was too mean to buy furniture) having refused to pay for a doctor.

HORRIBLE HUNT BALLS

WRITING IN HER SPLENDID 1926 MEMOIRS, Edwardian foxhunter Lady Augusta Fane lamented that after the Great War hunt balls became 'fairly horrible' with violent dances stimulated by too much alcohol. 'The ladies are swung off the ground with their legs in the air', sniffed Lady Augusta, who described an unfortunate moment at a ball in Derby when 'two ladies of title got entangled in each other's tiaras and were seen shaking and tossing their heads like angry stags in October, whilst the floor was strewn with diamonds, which were eagerly scrambled for by the people present'.

HUNTING DOES YOU GOOD

Water-Babies author Charles Kingsley was the classic foxhunting parson, who hunted with the Garth while he was vicar of Eversley in Hampshire. To Kingsley hunting was manly, which meant it was also Godly. Foxhunters were wholesome. 'With hounds, and in fast company, I never hear an oath', he assured a friend in 1857. Kingsley seldom attended meets for fear of being criticised for neglecting his spiritual duties. Instead he would go riding at about midday and just happen to fall in with the hunt.

Kingsley suffered from acute depression throughout his life, the only cure for which seemed to be hunting, fishing and shooting. In his 1867 novel *Yeast*, about foxhunters in rural England, Kingsley appears to be talking about himself when the hero, Lancelot Smith, declares: 'You complain that I waste my time in field-sports: how do you know I waste my time? I feel that the exercise of freedom, activity, foresight, daring, independent self-determination, even in a few minutes' burst across the country strengthens me in mind as well as body. Hunting does me good.'

Kingsley retired from the chase in his forties, partly due to pressure from people within the church who did not approve of hunting parsons, but mostly because he could not afford decent mounts – despite his fame, he made little money from his writing and his significant earnings came posthumously.

In a sad essay written after some friends had tried to drag him out hunting, he explained, 'My hunting days are over. Let it suffice that I have, in the days of my vanity, drunk delight of battle with my peers, far on the ringing plains of many a county, grass and forest, down and vale. No, my gallant friends. You know that I could ride, if I chose…But it is past two now and I have four old women to read to at three, and an old man to bury at four; and I think, on the whole, that you will respect me the more for going home and doing my duty. That I should like to see this fox fairly killed, or even fairly lost, I deny not. That I should like it as much as I can like any earthly and outward thing, I deny not. But sugar to one's bread and butter is not good; and if my winter garden represent the bread and butter then will fox-hunting stand to it in the relation of superfluous and unwholesome sugar; so farewell, and long may your noble sport prosper…'

Kingsley died in 1875 aged fifty-six, following an illness contracted during a lecture tour of the United States.

DO NOT RETALIATE

Advice from the Master of Foxhounds Association on how to have a happy day's hunting…

- ❧ All who follow hunting must be aware of other countryside users. People work at a wide variety of businesses in rural areas, and there is an increasing number of recreational and leisure users of the countryside. Other people's views must be taken into account and respected. Every effort must be made to avoid giving offence. Common courtesy is essential and must be granted to everyone – a simple 'please' or 'thank you' costs nothing.

- ❧ Every effort must be made to prevent hounds and followers from straying into places where they are not welcome, or onto roads and railways.

- ❧ The wishes of all landholders, no matter how small, must be respected. Never do anything that would be detrimental to agricultural interests.

- ❧ The aims of saboteurs are to disrupt hunting and provoke hunt followers. Confrontation with saboteurs must be avoided whenever possible and, in any event, followers must not retaliate whatever the provocation. Frequently saboteurs are breaking the law. You can help by recording details of vehicle registration numbers, taking photographic evidence, making identifications and listing times and places of incidents. Be prepared to make written notes and report incidents to an appropriate hunt official.

MISUNDERSTOOD

'For weeks he takes the field and does his best,
Tugged here and there, rough ridden, ripped with spurs,
Misunderstood, mishandled, over-stressed;
The mount of any fool that fate prefers.
Then one proud day he plays a leader's part
Across the green grass-lands,
Carrying a horseman with a gallant heart
And light and loving hands.'

Another Hireling, *by Will H. Ogilvie*

CHARGING AT FULL SPEED

LEICESTERSHIRE HUNTING COUNTRY in the nineteenth century, particularly the Quorn, was known for the bullfinch, a terrifying obstacle attempted by only the serious foxhunter. Here *The Sporting Magazine* describes the Leicestershire bullfinch of the 1850s:

'This is a quick-set hedge of, perhaps, fifty years' growth, with a ditch on one side or the other, and so high and strong that horses cannot clear it. The sportsman, however, charging straight into this at full speed, succeeds in getting to the other side, when the bushes close after him and his horse, and there is no more appearance of their transit than if a bird had hopped through. Horses, unaccustomed to these fences, seldom face them well at first; perhaps, the emulation which animates their riders, and the courage created in the noble animals themselves by the presence of hounds, would induce them to face such things at all.'

- The word 'bullfinch' is a corruption of 'bull fence'.

- Melton Mowbray swells would secretly dispatch their grooms at night to part-saw through the tallest, thickest hunt jumps and mark the weak spots with pieces of paper. The next day the rider could charge through unharmed, while uninitiated female onlookers marvelled at such bravery.

HARE BRAIN

ENGLAND'S MOST TALKED ABOUT MASTER was 'Mad' Jack Mytton (1796–1834), a Shropshire squre and professional nutcase, whose eccentricities were greatly embellished in a posthumous biography by the hunting journalist Nimrod who considered him a great character.

Like so many masters, Mytton, Master of the Albrighton, was a bit of a loony, but a lot more loony than the rest of 'em. 'A hare-brained votary of the Chase', is how one writer described him.

Endless so-called entertaining stories are told about this drunkard who must have actually been a trying man:

- He was expelled from Harrow and Westminster where he proved to be so stupid that his tutor's recommended reading was the Racing Calendar and the Stud Book.

- He set fire to his nightshirt to cure hiccups. Or the story went that he set fire to a friend's nightshirt to cure his friend's hiccups. Choose which ever version you like.

- On his way home from hunting one day he stopped at a farm which had a savage guard dog. The farmer warned Mytton not to go near it. Mytton grabbed the animal and bit it on the nose. The howling cur fled to its kennel and never barked at anybody in a red coat again.

- In pursuit of hounds, he rode his horse across the River Severn even though he couldn't swim.

- He used to ride his tame bear Nell around the drawing room at his Shropshire family seat Halston. The bear did not always see the funny side and once bit him on the leg.

- He got a horse-dealer hog-whimpering drunk and then put him in bed with two bulldogs and the bear. The horse-dealer's fate is unknown.

- On the plus side, Mytton was a surprisingly good farmer and and won prizes for his grain.

- He lost a fortune gambling. When told he shouldn't sell his estate because it had been in his family for five hundred years he replied, 'Then it is high time it should go out of it!'

• He became MP for Shrewsbury, but found the job boring and spent only thirty minutes in the House of Commons.

• He would drive his carriage at high speed at obstacles to see if it would turn over. His life was described as 'a series of suicide attempts'.

• He once galloped at full speed over a rabbit warren, to try whether or not his horse would fall, which, of course, it did.

• He robbed his friends while dressed as a masked highwayman.

• He was obsessed by clothes and owned 150 pairs of breeches.

• He contracted pneumonia, after going out one frozen night naked to shoot duck.

Mytton's problems may have stemmed from the fact that his father died when he was two and his mother spoiled him rotten. Having been expelled from both Westminster and Harrow he became an officer in the Hussars where he lost huge amounts at cards and billiards. He returned to his country estate and an income of £10,000 per year (around £750,000 today.) He got married aged twenty-three. His wife Harriet, daughter of a baronet, died a couple of years later. 'There can be no doubt that her death was accelerated, if not caused, by her husband's insane and cruel conduct,' remarked a contemporary.

That he was a great Master of Foxhounds there is no doubt. He led the Albrighton for five years, hunting five days a week. He was an exceptional, if manic, horseman. However, Nimrod pointed out he was not a great hound breeder: 'He allowed his packs to become such a queer mixture that they might have been intended to hunt stag, fox, or hare, or all three, for aught one could gather from their appearance'.

Eventually, Mytton's gambling losses became so great that the trustees at Halston threw him out for fear that the estate would have to be sold. After fleeing to France, Mytton returned, sodden with brandy, only to be thrown into debtor's jail where he died aged thirty-eight. An obituarist noted that the squire had brought 'ruin and degradation upon his ancient line'.

Mytton was succeeded by his son, also called Jack, who was just as bad and described as 'a devoted patron of the Turf, the Ring, and the dice-box, who when he had reached the length of his tether, sank into ignoble indigence'. Jack Jnr blew the lot. Upon his death aged fifty-three in 1875 Halston was sold to a Manchester industrialist.

ATTACKS ON HUNTING: A RANDOM RECENT HISTORY

1925. Hunting grandee Lord Willoughby de Broke MFH declares that anybody who is anti-hunting is anti-patriotic. 'If there be anyone who is temperamentally opposed to the sport, and would injure it if he could, he is hardly worth considering. His whole outlook would probably be anti-social and un-English.'

1934. Willoughby de Broke's 'un-English' point is proven when Reichsmarschall Hermann Goering bans hunting in Germany.

1949. Two anti-hunting bills are announced in Parliament. Backbencher Seymour Cock's private members bill wants to ban hare coursing and deer, badger and otter hunting. A second bill is aimed at foxhunting. The first is thrown out and second withdrawn. Several Labour MPs vote against the foxhunting ban because in some rural areas hunting is the only winter recreation for farm workers.

1953. Robert Churchward resigns as Master of the South Shropshire in 1953 and declares he is anti-blood sports. He publishes a pamphlet revealing the 'cruelties of hunting – all hunting for "sport" is organised torture, leading to murder'. He and his wife are shunned and receive abusive phone calls. Friends point out that Churchward has hunted all his life. The more charitable ones reckon he has suffered a nervous breakdown and has gone a bit odd.

1957. The Transport and General Worker's Union, like it is any of their business, describe hunting as 'distasteful to the British way of life'.

1964. A breakaway group from the League Against Cruel Sports, The Hunt Saboteurs Association is formed. They resort to tactics such as stringing piano wire at neck height in woodland in the hopes foxhunters might decapitate themselves. This organisation spawns another outfit called The Hunt Retribution Squad. With flat coldness a spokesman promises, 'At first we will just inflict injuries, which will increase in severity...the next stage will be to actually take a hunter out completely'. A League Against Cruel sports spokesman says, 'Someone who is willing to press a button that would blow away millions of innocent people is the same sort of person who would hunt a fox...'. This ludicrous claim prompts historian Jane Ridley to make the splendid remark: 'For them, men like the 10th Duke of Beaufort were nukes in fancy dress'.

1965. RSPCA member Vera Sheppard proposes an anti-foxhunting motion at the AGM and demands that hunts go drag hunting instead. *Horse & Hound* advises readers to pack out the RSPCA's meeting. The motion is soundly defeated by members such as the Duke of Beaufort and Marcus Kimball MP.

1967. Bloodsports again debated in Parliament and attempts made to ban hare coursing, but the bill is talked out by Kimball, who has become a hero in pro-hunting circles. The RSPCA try unsuccessfully to expel Kimball from the society.

1970s. Psychologist Hans Eysenck conducts a study of MFHs. He arrives at the stunning conclusion that MFHs tend to be 'conservative' and 'tough-minded' with a preference for capital punishment.

1981. The Greater London Council, led by Ken Livingston, cancels one of the most popular events at the Greater London Horse Show, the traditional appearance of hounds from the Surrey Union Hunt.

1982. The Cooperative Congress bans hunting on 38,000 acres of Coop land. About a dozen hunts affected mainly in the east Midlands and the South west. The Coop refuses to even look at a petition signed by 80,000 hunt supporters calling for a removal of the ban. (Note that the Coop did not consult their farm managers about banning

hunting; nor did they ban shooting on their land.)

1985. Labour-run Warwickshire County Council bans hunting on 45,000 acres of farm land.

1988. The League Against Cruel Sports fails to get hunting banned on the National Trust's 600,000 acres.

1997. Labour comes into power with a hunting ban in their electoral manifesto. Keen angler and avowed self-publicist Labour MP Michael Foster presents a bill to ban hunting with dogs. Prime Minister Tony Blair reportedly takes Foster aside and says, 'Oh for God's sake. I thought you were someone who concentrated on things that matter'. But Blair soon finds the threatened ban useful. It is a bone to toss to Labour's left-wing. The countryside reacts with a 125,000-strong pro-hunting rally in London's Hyde Park. *Guardian* journalist Polly Toynbee makes the prophetic remark, 'Hunting the toffs will become a tricky business and Labour may come to wish it had gone to earth on this one... are all Labour MPs so thoroughly intimidated by the animal rights lobby?' The Countryside Alliance is formed to fight the proposed ban.

1998. Over 400,000 protest by joining the Countryside March through London.

1999. Retired civil servant Lord Burns launches Government inquiry into hunting with dogs. The Burns committee famously concludes that hunting with dogs 'seriously compromises' the welfare of the fox. Burns adds that there is not sufficient evidence to suggest that hunting is cruel. Despite this, Labour forges ahead with plans for a ban. 100,000 join pro-hunt rallies throughout the UK.

2000. Labour Deputy Prime Minister John Prescott launches an unnecessary attack on the 'contorted faces' of the Countryside Alliance.

2001. Graham Sirl, senior executive of the League Against Cruel Sports, quits the League in disgust declaring that a ban on stag hunting would be bad for animal welfare.

2002. Miles Cooper, who has worked for the Hunt Saboteurs Association, the League Against Cruel Sports, the International Fund for Animal Welfare and the Campaign for Protectionof Hunted Animals, quits the animal rights business saying that a hunting ban could cause wild mammal welfare to 'degenerate into chaos'.

2003 Actress Annette Crosbie is named President of the League Against Cruel Sports. She describes herself as 'impatient, intolerant, judgmental, tactless – I'm not very nice, I'm really not'.

2004. September: the Metropolitan Police take their truncheons to 10,000 noisy, pro-hunting protestors in Parliament Square. Otis Ferry and friends storm the House of Commons. November: After 700 hours of debate and at huge cost, the Hunting Act is passed 339 to 155 votes and receives Royal Assent. Labour activists regard this as payback to Conservative Britain for everything from the crushing of the miners' strike by Thatcher to preserving 'traditional British values'.

2005. February. The Hunting Act becomes law. On the first day of the ban more than 270 hunts are riding out and ninety-four foxes are killed as a result of 'hunting within the law'. The police maintain a low profile; most policemen regard the new hunting law as an ass. At one Midlands hunt a single panda car arrives with a copper who, as hounds set off, remarks to the Master, 'That looks fun. Wouldn't mind trying it myself.' But not all policemen are pro-hunting. In September 2005 gamekeeper Charlotte Denis, twenty, is arrested for wearing a 'Bollocks To Blair' T-shirt at the Midlands Game Fair in Staffordshire on the grounds that the slogan might offend elderly people. She is later released without charge. The Countryside Alliance comment, 'Surely the police have better things to do with their time than protect the Prime Minister's modesty.'

2006. It is estimated that the number of people engaging in

hunting has risen by eleven per cent. Many people are now following hunts as a way of saying 'up yours' to New Labour.

2007. The antis make much of the fact that fifty-six people have been found guilty of breaking the hunting law. However, it emerges that twenty of these convictions were on Merseyside, seven of which were for hunting rats without the landowner's permission. Most of the others were prosecuted for hunting hares and foxes without the landowner's permission, all of which would have been against the law before the Hunting Act. Only three convictions have anything to do with registered hunts.

2009. Since the hunting ban has come into effect 325 registered hunts in England and Wales have carried out 70,000 hunting days. Hunting is carried out legally by either laying a scent or by using a pack to flush a fox or another mammal to a bird of prey and by hound exercise. Meanwhile, Prime Minister Gordon demonstrates his concern for the countryside by appointing Dan Norris, one of the most vociferous supporters of the Hunting Act, as Minister for Rural Affairs. Only recently Norris has joined animal rights activists outside his constituency to 'monitor' the Blackmore and Sparkford Vale Hunt. Considering himself aloof from those he regards as scum, like a

feudal lord of olden times, he refuses to speak to hunt supporters. To ensure the countryside really appreciates what Labour is doing, Gordon Brown appoints fellow Scot Jim Fitzpatrick as Minister for Food, Farming and Environment. Fitzpatrick has excellent credentials for such a post in a Labour Government – he is a vegetarian and represents an East London constituency. Interestingly, Michael Foster, the MP who first proposed the ban, has long ago faded into obscurity...

The Present: At time of writing Britain has a Liberal Conservative coalition government who have promised a free vote on the Hunting Act, though it is doubtful that there would be enough pro-hunting MPs to carry it through.

The future: Uncertain